William Fairweather

From the Exile to the Advent

William Fairweather

From the Exile to the Advent

ISBN/EAN: 9783743310858

Manufactured in Europe, USA, Canada, Australia, Japa

Cover: Foto ©Thomas Meinert / pixelio.de

Manufactured and distributed by brebook publishing software
(www.brebook.com)

William Fairweather

From the Exile to the Advent

HANDBOOKS

FOR

BIBLE CLASSES

AND PRIVATE STUDENTS

EDITED BY

PROFESSOR MARCUS DODS, D.D.

AND

REV ALEXANDER WHYTE, D.D.

FROM THE EXILE TO THE ADVENT

EDINBURGH

T. & T. CLARK, 38 GEORGE STREET

1895

ASSYRIA

AND THE ADJACENT LANDS

TO

THE ADVENT

BY

REV. WILLIAM FAIRWEATHER, M.A.

KIRKCALDY

—➤◄—

EDINBURGH

T. & T. CLARK, 38 GEORGE STREET

1895

CONTENTS

BOOK I

THE EXILE AND THE RETURN, B.C. 588-538

BOOK II

THE PERSIAN PERIOD, B.C. 537-333

BOOK V

THE ASMONEAN DYNASTY, B.C. 135–63

CHAPTER I

BOOK VI

THE ROMAN PERIOD, B.C. 63–4

CHAPTER I

BOOK I

THE EXILE AND THE RETURN, B.C. 588–538

CHAPTER I

The Epoch of the Exile

1. The Name and what it covers.—The name *Exile*, when used without qualification, cannot be said to give a very correct idea of the historical relations of the period under review. It is an improvement on the designation so long in use—that of the *Captivity*; but even when we distinguish between the Assyrian and the Babylonian Exile it is very inadequate, and does the history no justice. *Deportation* is perhaps the word that best conveys a right conception of what happened to the Israelitish people at this crisis. It was a favourite principle of Eastern despotism to remove large numbers of people from their native settlements to some region within the domains of the conquering power. This weakened the alien and strengthened the empire; while the mixture of blood tended also to the spread of general culture. The dregs of the population were usually left behind. It was upon the nobility, the youth, and the intelligence of a vanquished community that the victors liked to prey. The application of this principle by Nebuchadnezzar to the Hebrew nation brought about the condition of things known as *the Exile*. It will be necessary to keep in view the following facts :—
(1) The deportation of the Ten Tribes to Assyria, about B.C. 740.

What became of these tribes is a question which has been the theme of much fruitless discussion. May they not have returned to Jerusalem with their fellow - countrymen of Judah? The general number who did so return is stated at 42,000, while the particulars as given in Ezra amount to only 29,000. The difference of 13,000 may very well have been composed of persons belonging to the other tribes. (2) The name Exile, however, is usually associated with an event vastly more important for Israelitish history, although directly affecting only a minority of the nation, viz. the downfall of the kingdom of Judah, the destruction of the temple at Jerusalem, and the carrying away of the inhabitants to Babylon. The position of Judea between Egypt and Babylonia was a very critical one. It was the natural battlefield over which swept the ever-shifting tide of conquest. In the course of events the Judeans had become tributary to the growing empire of Babylon, and vainly thought with the help of Egypt to throw off their vassalage. The end of their abortive attempts in this direction was the deportation under Jehoiakim, in B.C. 598. After plundering the temple, Nebuchadnezzar took away as prisoners to Babylon the boy-king and his Court, and the cream of the people, including Ezekiel and many other priests. (3) Ten years later, in B.C. 588, came the bitter end, in the form of another and more complete deportation. Zedekiah, who had been appointed king over the impoverished remnant, weakly allowed himself to be drawn into a confederacy with Egypt. This proved his ruin ; for Nebuchadnezzar once more marched against Judea and laid siege to Jerusalem. Zedekiah now sent for Jeremiah, who had been cast into prison for maintaining that the siege would be successful. Again he desired to know from his lips the message of Jehovah. It was still the same, and the infatuated king sent the faithful prophet back to his cell. Within the year Jerusalem was taken and destroyed by fire. Most of the people were carried to Babylon. No one was left who was worth removing. The fate of the king himself was a very sad one. After seeing his sons slain, he had his own eyes put out, and ended his miserable life in a Babylonian prison. The Jews kept alive the recollection of this calamity by special days of fasting. As for the miserable remnant in Judea, over whom Gedaliah had been appointed governor, we find that they soon fled to Egypt for fear of the Chaldees. The personal history of Jeremiah loses itself in this sea of troubles. All we know is that he was carried by force to Egypt, where he continued to assert the divine mission of Nebuchadnezzar, and his coming conquest of the very land to which his poor countrymen had fled for refuge.

2. **Significance of the Exile.**—With the destruction of the Holy City a great turning-point in the national development is reached. The Exile is like a line bisecting the history, all that goes before having a well-marked character of its own, and all that follows taking colour from this signally important event. Hitherto there had been a feeling in Jewish hearts that even amid their many defections from His service, Jehovah was still with them. Had they suffered calamities? The Holy City had remained nevertheless, its walls defended by His power. And was not their great temple the visible embodiment of the divine presence? But now came the rude awakening. They had been "haughty because of God's holy mountain," and with one fell blow the source of their pride was swept away. The earlier bands of exiles went forth no doubt with lighter hearts than did the later. They had thought matters would right themselves again, as they had always done before; but consternation must have seized on them when they heard that their countrymen whom they had left behind were also on their way to Babylon, with the ashes of Jerusalem—walls, palaces, and temple together—smouldering in the rear. Everything distinctive of God's Israel was now wiped out. Monarchy had failed. The kings had been weighed in the balances and found wanting. Under them the people had sunk deeper than ever into corruption and idolatry. The noble part played by the prophets at this juncture stands in brightest

contrast to the miserable character of the later Jewish kings. The only exception to the general worthlessness of these men was Josiah ; his successors were all more or less like Zedekiah, of whom Josephus says that he was "a despiser of justice and of his duty."

3. The Rationale of the Exile.—Why was there such a thing at all ? It was the execution of the divine judgment which had long been threatening the chosen people. The cloud had been gathering and thickening on every side. Egypt on the south, and the newly-consolidated empire of Chaldea on the north, were both ready to swallow up the little Israelitish kingdom that lay between. There is something of an analogy in the present position of Bulgaria in relation to the great neighbouring powers of the Slavs and Teutons. Add to this that the Israelites were harassed by their hereditary foes, the Philistines and Edomites, and by the plundering banditti of the desert, and there can be no dubiety regarding the outward occasion of an event whose real inner cause lay in the unfaithfulness to God of the Israelitish nation. The degeneracy extended in considerable measure even to prophets and priests; while, as for the great body of the people, they had given themselves up to idolatry and worldliness. Josiah's reform—the only bright spot in their later history—had not been radical enough. This was proved by the rampant wickedness that sprang up after the good king's death. Heathen abominations were substituted for the worship of Jehovah. Moloch and Ashtaroth had become the favourite divinities of a sunken people ; they had even embraced the animal worship of Egypt, and did obeisance to reptiles and creeping things. The whole framework of society was rotten, from the Court downwards. Home life, public life, and religious life were equally corrupt. The day of visitation, so often proclaimed by the prophets, and as often unheeded by the people, had now come.

It would, however, be a mistake to regard the judgments meted out to Israel as merely punitive ; they were educative as well, and intended to fit them for their unique divine calling and destiny. From them was to arise the Messiah, the Man of His right hand, whom Jehovah was to exalt to be a Prince and a Saviour. But they were not yet ready for this. The nation must be purified by a complete severance from the scene and associations of a long course of evil-doing. In political servitude they must regain spiritual freedom, and in a strange land and amid unwelcome surroundings they must revert to the love of truth and righteousness, and to the practice of faith and holiness. We must therefore view the Exile as a great forward step in the development of Israel's religion. Their special mission as a nation could never be fulfilled so long as they clung in selfish isolation to the forms of a material temple.

Only by the severest measures could they be brought back to their true position as the chosen of God. The punitive instrument arose in the person of Nebuchadnezzar, whom the prophets speak of accordingly as Jehovah's "servant." God made the policy of the earthly monarch subservient to His own: Nebuchadnezzar needed citizens at the same time that God wanted a purified people. The King of Babylon and his empire were simply the means He was pleased to use for the accomplishment of His own designs. And what designs of His were being wrought out in the history of Israel? No Christian needs to be told that in the fall of Jerusalem there was the death of a seed-corn that carried with it a fulness of power not yet exhausted, but working on wherever the gospel is preached.

The crushing nature of the Babylonian yoke had now become only too apparent. By degrees it had advanced until the enemy's heel was fairly upon Judah's neck. The epoch of the Exile lasted, strictly speaking, little more than half a century, the seventy years of Jeremiah being reckoned from the fourth year of Jehoiakim, or the first of Nebuchadnezzar. Yet even half a century is an important period in a nation's history, and it can well be conceived that half a century in exile—the peculiar case of the Hebrews—must have been particularly so.

CHAPTER II

The Home of the Exiles

1. General Plan of Babylon.—Ancient Babylon was in many respects the most remarkable city the world has ever seen. The great monarch whose creation it was, being now at rest from war, resolved to apply his mind to the task of strengthening and adorning his capital—a task which he executed with characteristic energy up to the day when he made the proud boast, "Is not this great Babylon which I have built?" In trying to form some idea of the magnificence of this old-world metropolis, we are thrown back upon such accounts as have come down to us from ancient history, for the glory of Babylon has long since passed away. These accounts are not numerous, and even when they were written Babylon was on the wane. The decipherment of the cuneiform inscriptions has brought to light many important facts which supplement, and to some extent correct, the historical statements. Both alike corroborate, however, what is said in Scripture as to the hugeness of the city, and the immensity of the scale on which everything connected with it was contrived and carried out. Situated on a vast level plain, with the Euphrates flowing through it and dividing it into two almost equal sections, ancient Babylon took the form of a perfect square. As to the size of this square, our chief authorities—Herodotus and Ctesias—differ considerably, the one probably giving the measurement from the outer, and the other that from the inner wall; but the lowest figure given by any writer of antiquity compels us to think of a city four times as large as London. The plan was that of Nineveh, but Nebuchadnezzar resolved to make Babylon an improvement upon Nineveh. Having finished the wall begun by his father, he built another inside of it so as to render the place impregnable. That these "walls" were really huge mounds or artificial hills thrown round the city, we might infer from their height, which, on the lowest reckoning, was more than 300 feet; and from their breadth, which was such that six chariots could drive abreast upon the top. The Chinese Wall is perhaps the only work of man that can be compared with them in magnitude. On each side of the square were 25 gates of solid brass; and placed at irregular intervals round the wall were 250 towers, each raised above the general altitude. According to Herodotus, the gates on the opposite sides of the square enclosure were so placed that the streets ran from gate to gate, each of them being 15 miles long. This would give in all 50 streets of that length, 25 running in one direction, and being crossed at right angles by an equal number. There were also four streets built on one side only, immediately adjoining the walls. The whole city was therefore composed of 676 squares, each 2¼ miles in compass. The houses, to the height of three or four storeys, were built on the outside of the squares, a space within being left for gardens and general cultivation. Probably from sanitary considerations, and as a safeguard against fire, there were also gaps left between the houses; indeed, the greater part of the city cannot have been occupied by buildings at all. A large proportion of its huge area was laid out in fields and gardens, so that in case of siege the inhabitants could grow their own provisions within the walls. Such was the general plan of Babylon, not more vast than it was exact. It was a bold conception, and boldly carried out. Nature supplied no fortresses, but the genius and energy of Nebuchadnezzar made them. Huge trenches were dug both inside and outside the walls. Herodotus tells us how they set to work: "As fast as they dug the moat, the soil which they got from the cutting was made into bricks, and when a sufficient number were completed they baked the bricks in kilns. Then they proceeded to build, and began with bricking the borders of the moat, after which they proceeded to construct the wall itself, using throughout for their cement hot bitumen, and interposing a layer of wattled reeds at every course of bricks."

2

Thus there was produced one of the seven wonders of the world.

2. **Architecture.**—Among the many remarkable buildings in Babylon, Bab-bel, the Temple of Bel (i.e. *gate of God*), carried the palm. Upon a base of 200 square yards it rose in terrace-fashion to the extraordinary height of 600 feet—a record that eclipses the magnificence of any cathedral ever erected.[1] This was the ancient shrine of the Babylonians, believed by many to have been the actual tower of Babel. For long it had been the great seat of paganism in Mesopotamia, and was designated "the terrace tower, the everlasting house, the temple of the seven lights of the earth." It was here that Nebuchadnezzar deposited the sacred vessels carried away from Jerusalem. The wealth stored up in it is stated in figures that appear quite fabulous. Before the magnitude and gorgeousness of this temple the beholder must have stood amazed. Its seven stages were dedicated to as many planets, with appropriate colouring,—gold for the Sun, silver for the Moon, azure for Mercury, and so on. Upon the place of honour at the summit was the sanctuary of Nebo, referred to in the prophetic song over the fall of Babylon, "Bel sinketh down, Nebo stoopeth." No fewer than forty-two kings had feared to complete this tower, after the destruction that attended its first erection, but Nebuchadnezzar has proudly put it on record that *he* did not hesitate to undertake the work. Another of the most notable buildings in Babylon—erected, too, say the historians, in the incredibly short period of fifteen days—was the Palace Royal. It stood within ample grounds, and was surrounded by a wall seven miles in circumference. Externally and internally the palace itself was of great magnificence; it could boast of "many chambers and lofty towers," and lacked nothing in the way of beautiful fabrics or splendid painting. But the city was chiefly remarkable for its "hanging gardens." These were

---

[1] The towers of Cologne Cathedral, which are the loftiest in Europe, rise to an altitude of 512 feet.

raised in huge successive terraces, supported by great arches and strengthened by thick walls. After they were laid out and planted, the effect was that of beautiful and extensive pleasure-grounds, with hill and dale, flowers and fountains, trees and grass. Nebuchadnezzar had married a Median princess, and "to gratify her herein," says Prideaux, "was the reason of erecting this monstrous work of vanity."

It is impossible here to make any detailed reference to the intricate and ingenious system of river-banks, bridges, tunnels, canals, and artificial lakes by which this unique city was watered, connected, safeguarded, and adorned. "Of the great waters,"— so reads an inscription of Nebuchadnezzar,—"like the waters of the ocean, I made use abundantly." Under his magic hand the inland capital became thus a sort of floating emporium to which traders from every quarter were attracted. Whatever could be done by an unlimited supply of bricks and bitumen, for these were furnished by the clay soil and the river springs ; whatever could be achieved by an equally unlimited supply of labour, for that had been obtained from the wars ; whatever an iron will and a great genius could accomplish, for both were united in Nebuchadnezzar,—all this combined to produce ancient Babylon.

3. **Education.**—The Babylonians were a literary people. Books were plentiful, and, being stored in public libraries, were accessible to all. The great bulk of them were written upon clay tablets, although in some instances papyrus would seem to have been used. Schools for both sexes were established ; and, notwithstanding the difficulty of acquiring the ideographic system, a large proportion of the inhabitants could read and write. More advanced instruction was also given. History and geography were both subjects of study, and a knowledge of several foreign languages (such as Aramaic, Assyrian, and even Hebrew, was deemed indispensable to a liberal education. Borsippa is mentioned by Strabo in terms which justify us in thinking of it as

a famous university seat. That many availed themselves of these facilities for learning is beyond doubt. Who has not heard of the wise men of Babylon, the astrologers, the sorcerers, and the magicians? In the motley society of the Chaldean Empire they formed a most powerful and influential order; for the education of the country, its politics, and its religion were all controlled by them. They were the leaders of thought, and the representatives of culture; the greatest force in civilising, the main factor in developing, the complex national life. Counsellors to the king, and fathers to the people, they were looked upon as the embodiment of the wisdom of the age. Whole treatises on grammar, mathematics, geography, natural history, astronomy, law, and government have already been deciphered from those curious tablets of clay on which these Chaldean sages were wont to chronicle the results of their observation and research. We owe to them the beginnings of astronomical science. They constructed a zodiac with its twelve constellations, and a sphere on which our own is largely modelled. To them we owe also the invention of the sun-dial, and our division of time. They could calculate eclipses, and were diligent in recording their observations of them. On taking Babylon, Alexander the Great came into possession of a catalogue of eclipses observed there during nearly two thousand years. We still possess the records of some of them, and they are of infinite value both to the astronomer and chronologist. Their habit of transmitting the outcome of their united labour from generation to generation accounts for the wonderful progress made by these old-world star-gazers. We do not know the names of the giants among them; they were a body engaged in a common enterprise for the advancement of knowledge, and were nobly indifferent to personal fame.

4. Religion of the Babylonians.—This was intimately connected with their scientific teaching; the two were, in fact, one. Their mathematical calculations fostered the scientific spirit, but their star-gazing induced likewise a spirit of contemplation and religious awe. They looked up to those glittering worlds for the power that is divine, and saw in them the outward manifestation of Deity. Particularly was this the case as regards the seven out-standing heavenly bodies—the sun and moon, and the five planets then known to them. The Semitic races in general appear to have been addicted to this nature-worship, which centred for the most part in the celestial bodies, and which usually goes by the name of Sabeism. Once the stars are viewed as divine beings, with the attributes of intelligence and power, it is an easy step to ascribe to them the ordering of human destiny. Their every motion and change of aspect came to be interpreted as fraught with good or evil to the children of men, whose entire lot was thus conceived as being plainly written in the sky, if only it could be read. None but the most gifted spirits could hope to acquire this power. And where were these to be found save in the priesthood? Who else could penetrate into the secrets of heaven? A powerful weapon was thus put into the hands of the priests as the accredited medium for ascertaining the will of the gods. Such a system was, of course, polytheistic, although the priests' language showed a tendency towards the grander con-ception of one Supreme Power, unseen and inaccessible, to whom these lower divinities, so regular in their motions, were under law. They spoke of the forces of nature as emanations of God ; but they had no thought of a *creation*, and their idea of one Almighty Power was at the best cloudy and obscure. On the other hand, they went on dividing and subdividing their numerous so-called emanations, ascribing different functions to each, till one gets lost in trying to wade through the mazes of their groups of deities. Each member of their pantheon had many temples all over the land, every town having its own favourite divinity. Much atten-tion was paid also to the art of *divination*, which was applied to the most meagre details of life, until life must have been made ridiculous. Omens were drawn from the rustling of trees, the form of lightnings, the flight of birds, the smoke of sacrifices, etc.

And thus, besides the star-watchers and their astronomy, there were the sorcerers with their incantations, and the soothsayers with their fortune-telling ; and in these we have descending grades of these clever sons of Babylon. In so far as they led the way in pure scientific observation they deserve our gratitude ; but we can hardly be thankful for the mass of absurdities they contrived to hand down along with it. The very word *magic*, and many of the lingering superstitions that still pervade ignorant people of nearly every nation, we probably owe to these ancient wizards. With all their acquirements, their science was a strange compound of accurate knowledge and superstitious lore. If our leading scientists were to dabble in witchcraft, and to act as fortune-tellers and interpreters of dreams, we should have some sort of parallel to the part played by these wise men of the East. Their sincerity was probably on a level with that of the Roman augurs, who laughed to one another in the streets ! The better side of their activity is seen in some of their hymns. The jumbling of religions that took place in Babylonia, and the development of new creeds out of fragments of old ones, produced in the later days of the empire the astonishing result that the hymns and prayers of the oldest settlers in Chaldea, though still addressed to the Sun, began to take on a more spiritual and sometimes almost biblical aspect. For example, a conjuror prays thus for his patient: " O Sun, leave not my uplifted hands unregarded ! Eat his food, refuse not his sacrifice. . . . May his sin at thy behest be forgiven, his misdeed be forgotten ! May he recover from his illness ! . . . " [1] In this petition there is evidently the thought of trouble being the punishment of sin. There are also, in some hymns, deep outpourings of penitence. Perhaps we can best account for this advance in spirituality on the supposition that it was the reflection of the silent but subtle influence of the Hebrews in their midst.

Such were the outward surroundings, and such the intellectual

[1] See Ragozin's *Chaldea*, chap. iii.

and religious conditions, amid which the exiled Jews were called to live, and work, and wait.

CHAPTER III

THE STORY OF THE EXILE

1. The Course of Empire.— There never was a more dazzling empire than that of Babylonia ; but if it was brilliant, it was also short-lived.   She had risen on the ruins of Assyria ; but so had the kingdom of the Medes and Persians, and they were prepared to contest with her the supremacy of Asia.   While weaklings and conspirators were passing from one to another the sceptre of Nebuchadnezzar, the founder of the "silver empire" which he had beheld in his dream, Cyrus the Persian was startling the world by his successes in war.   Nabonidus, who had usurped the throne of Babylon, began to strengthen its fortifications in view of a possible attack ; and as he had married a daughter of Nebuchadnezzar, he made his son Belshazzar, while yet a boy, partner of his throne, in order to curry favour with the populace. This is that Belshazzar of whom we read in the Book of Daniel, and whose tragic death sounded the knell of Babylon's greatness. It was a night of revelry with him and his courtiers, and while they were madly feasting and fancying themselves secure, Cyrus as God's anointed appeared within the gates.

The real supremacy of Babylon had died with Nebuchadnezzar. His successor, Nabonidus, was at first disposed to welcome Cyrus because he had crushed the Median King Astyages.   Little did he think that the warlike Elamite regarded his exploits up to this point as merely preliminary to the acquisition of Babylon itself.   But in time the designs of Cyrus became unmistakable, and Nabonidus resorted to strong defensive measures.   Hitherto

Cyrus had gradually been getting command of the outworks ; now he was to strike at the citadel. This was an ambitious programme, and it took him almost a decade to go through with it ; but between fighting and scheming he succeeded at last, to the great delight of the exiled Jews, who had watched his campaign with a wistful interest begotten of keenest expectation. The decisive event was a battle fought in Accad (south-eastern Chaldea) in B.C. 539. The Babylonians were put to rout, and the people of the province went over to the flag of Cyrus, whose religious toleration made him a not unwelcome ruler. From this to Nebuchadnezzar's throne there was but a single step. The people did not choose to make use of their unrivalled means of resistance, and, without a blow struck on either side, the city changed its sovereign. The unfortunate Nabonidus died soon after in prison, and Cyrus wore the Chaldean crown.

2. **Inner Life of the Jews in Babylon.** — (1) *Social.* — The writings of Jeremiah and Ezekiel make it clear that the condition of the exiles was not one of great oppression.[1] It cannot be compared with the tyranny their fathers endured in Egypt, nor even with the silly persecution still meted out to their descendants in some parts of Europe. Many of them would doubtless have to toil in the brickworks of Babylon, and a certain contingent would likely go to swell the imperial army. But the great body of the people were allowed to settle in clans, and to possess their own houses and plots of land (Ezek. iii. 24, xxxiii. 30). The only restriction to which they were subject was that they were obliged to remain where they were. The social framework of Judah was in large measure transplanted to Babylon. Though in reality prisoners, the Jews were treated as settlers, their ancient tribal system being still recognised. Several of them were taken into the palace itself to fill important offices of State. The prince of the house of Judah, though imprisoned by Nebuchadnezzar, was set at liberty by his son, and made to rank higher than any other

[1] Cf. Jer. xxix. 5 sqq.

captive king. The Talmud also asserts that they marked out one of their number as head of the captivity; and we know from the genealogies they were so careful to keep, that they were never in any doubt as to who was heir to David's crown.

(2) *Religious.*—They lived for the most part in the enjoyment of perfect religious liberty. The well-known exception of Nebuchadnezzar's edict, by which all were ordered to bow down before the image of Bel, is more apparent than real. It was more a political affair than a religious, and no foreign cult had anything to fear from Nebuchadnezzar so long as it did not imply hostility to the State. The Jews had still the services of their priesthood, and could observe, so far as was possible without the temple, the ceremonies of their law. A new importance was attached to the rite of circumcision, and to the observance of the Sabbath, as bonds of religious unity. No animal sacrifices could meanwhile be offered, but no outward circumstances could prevent them from offering the better sacrifice of prayer. They got into the habit, therefore, of assembling on the Sabbath for prayer and the reading of the word; and there can be no doubt that the great institution of the synagogue, which has played so important a part in all their subsequent history, was a product of the Exile. There is also a tradition of an academy having been founded for the study of the Scriptures as they then possessed them, and in this academy such men as Ezra and his coadjutors are supposed to have been trained. Four special days of fasting[1] were instituted in commemoration respectively of the unhappy day when the siege was begun; of the Chaldean entry into Jerusalem; of the destruction of the city and temple; and of the assassination of Gedaliah the governor. By careful attention to such legal observances as were not bound up with the Holy Land, and by these new enactments, the place of the Levitical worship was to some extent filled up.

(3) *Literary.*—During the Exile the *literary* activity of the

[1] Zech. viii. 19.

Israelites was very considerable. That they were intellectually quickened by their new surroundings there can be no doubt.[1] The crisis at which they had arrived naturally produced several prophetic books. After the deportation by Nebuchadnezzar, Jeremiah, who remained in the land until the seventh month, arranged and partly composed the work which bears his name. Part of the Book of Ezekiel falls within this period, and perhaps the prophet gave its final shape to the whole only towards the end of his life. The little Book of Obadiah also must be ascribed to this epoch, although it bears no trace of having been written in Babylonia. Above all, the marvellous collection of writings appended to the Book of Isaiah, and forming in our Bibles chaps. xl.–lxvi. of that work, were distinctly, for the most part, the product of the Exile. The high-water mark of Hebrew prophecy is reached in these oracles of a great prophet whose name we do not know. It is a somewhat remarkable fact that the finest creation of Hebrew poetry—the Book of Job—should also be anonymous. Although its date cannot be positively fixed, many scholars assign it likewise to the exilic period. That some of the Psalms were written in Babylon is highly probable. Nor was the important field of history neglected, for it is practically certain that the latest redaction of the Books of Kings took place during the Exile.[2] And although vexed questions are still debated with regard to the books collectively composing "the law," it can scarcely be maintained that the Hexateuch (i.e. the Pentateuch and Joshua) had taken final shape prior to the captivity. In respect of the general body of Hebrew literature, the period of the Exile contributed at least its own share.

---

[1] "Literary activity is one of the consolations of captives, prisoners, and exiles. Bunyan wrote the *Pilgrim's Progress* in Bedford jail; Spenser's *Faery Queen* was composed mainly in an Irish wilderness, and was thus, as the author tells us, 'the fruit of savage soil.' With books written under such conditions, none can compare for sweetness, beauty, and calm, solemn dignity. How much of the best Book do we owe to the exiles of Babylon!"
—Bruce, *Apologetics*, p. 266.

[2] Cf. 2 Kings xxv. 27.

(4) *Material.*—The mild treatment they received was not in every way an advantage to the Jewish exiles. Probably if they had had to endure persecution it would have been better for them. As it was, many of them got to love only too well the fertile plains to which they had been transported. The vast majority were able to live in comfort, and some appear to have amassed wealth. The old propensity to idolatry was not rooted out of them in spite of all that had occurred. The sensuous worship, the unbridled luxury, and in particular the stirring commercial life of Babylon, proved to such a temptation too strong to be resisted. And of course, in proportion as the idea of abandoning the fields they had tilled, and the houses they had built, became distasteful to them, their wish to return to Judea became a diminishing quantity. In many cases they lapsed into heathenism altogether, and in this sad fact we may recognise the secret of the bitter scorn with which the great prophet of the Exile exposes the foolishness of serving idols. To this degeneracy, however, there were not a few noble exceptions. There was a faithful remnant in whom the ardour of religious patriotism began to glow as it had never done before. These realised their calling, and pursued their religion with a power and purity begotten of adversity. The true Israelite could never be reconciled to Babylon. "To eat defiled bread among the Gentiles" was repulsive to him. Exile from Canaan was in itself the essence of misery; to be deprived of the temple was nearly equivalent to being cast off by the Lord. And thus, while the more worldly-minded Jews were making up their minds to settle in Babylon, the more faithful of the exiles kept aloof from heathen habits and sympathies, and clung to their own worship, and the hope of restoration to their own land. For them no amount of material wealth could remove the bitterness of captivity. They had the consciousness that God had chosen them for an exalted destiny, and the thought that the working out of this had meanwhile been checked, was in itself a grief sufficient to swallow up every joy. "They wept when they

remembered Zion." Goldsmith might have drawn from their experience his picture of "the pensive exile bending with his woe." As the years passed by they felt ever more keenly that they "were lying under a sort of vast interdict," and breathed with growing intensity the vow, "If I forget thee, O Jerusalem, let my right hand forget her cunning."

The conditions of life became harder for the exiles after Nebuchadnezzar's death. For one thing, the stability of the empire was no longer what it had been. The removal by Nabonidus of all local deities to the temples of the gods of Babylon had produced widespread disaffection. Foreign settlers and native priests were equally offended—the one class because of the dishonour done to their gods, and the other because of the inroad made upon their time-honoured religious usages. The Chaldeans, moreover, could not but see that these Hebrews viewed the situation with feelings very different from their own. To them the fall of Babylon would be a welcome relief; and when they had to take their share in fortifying their house of bondage, they would no doubt show that the task was not to their taste. The appointed period of their exile had nearly run its course. Some were impatient to be free—too impatient, seeing God had promised their deliverance. The result was seen in mutual hatred between them and their temporary masters. The Chaldeans tightened their grip upon the Jews; the Jews waited eagerly and hopefully for the discomfiture of the Chaldeans.

3. **The Agency of the Prophets.**—During this crisis the prophets had a twofold mission to discharge, for through them Jehovah sent His message both to the Jews and to the heathen. The great prophets of the time were Jeremiah, Ezekiel, Second Isaiah, and Daniel. Now that kings were no more, and the priests could not discharge their more important functions, the leadership of the people naturally devolved upon the prophets. What, then, was their combined God-given message to their own countrymen? *Serve the Lord, and trust Him to make "Chaldea a spoil," and*

*bring you back to your land, that as a purified people you may be
fitted for all His will.*

The tearful and high-souled Jeremiah, whose warning voice had
been unheeded in Jerusalem, but the truth of whose words had
been proved by the judgment which had overtaken them, now
wrote a letter of comfort and good cheer, full also of loving and
sagacious counsel, to the exiles of Babylon. He bade them pay
no heed to the dreams of the false prophets who had already
deceived them ; urged them to live quietly in the city of their
captivity, building houses and planting gardens ; and exhorted
them to seek the Lord with all their heart in prayer, for His
thoughts towards them were thoughts of peace and not of
evil, and in seventy years He would turn away their bondage
(Jer. xxix. 5–14).

But in addition to the written letter, they were favoured with the
guidance of the living voice. One day "as Ezekiel was among the
captives by the river of Chebar, the heavens were opened, and he
saw visions of God." To him the meaning of recent calamities
became perfectly plain, and he spent the days of his captivity by
the waters in expounding it to the people. Everything earthly
had gone down under them ; the prophet now put it to them
whether there was not something better for them to set their
hearts upon, even an eternal spiritual good. He set before them
the vision of the true Zion, the ideal holy commonwealth, having
the imperishable glory of the city of God (Ezek. viii. 3, 4), and
with the book of life for its burgess-roll. Jehovah would raise up
for them a plant of renown, and they should endure the shame of
the heathen no more (xxxiv. 29). Let them only bear their exile
aright ; let them fence themselves in from the heathen by observing the ceremonial law (xliv. 9, 23), and especially by hallowing
the Sabbaths (xliv. 24). In due time Jehovah would gather His
scattered sheep, and feed them upon the mountains of Israel by
the rivers (xxxiv. 13). A new heart also would He give to His
people, so that they should walk in His ways (xxxvi. 26, 27).

Second Isaiah, the perfervid evangelist of the Old Testament, co-operated with Ezekiel in assuring the exiles that there was no cause for despondency. The Lord's anointed was at hand (Isa. xliv. 28), the days of bondage were practically over. The king of Babylon and his golden city would soon become a proverb in the mouths of those whom he had oppressed (Isa. xiv. 4).[1] Go ye out of the midst of her (Isa. lii. 2), and "say ye, The Lord hath redeemed His servant Jacob" (Isa. xlviii. 20). Such was the luminous voice of prophecy to the down-trodden servants of Jehovah.

What Jeremiah sought to accomplish by his writings, and Ezekiel by his winged words, Daniel effected still more powerfully by the influence of his life. Promises and symbols alone could hardly sustain the faith of the exiles. But in the position and devoted example of Daniel they had a standing reply to all their doubts and fears. It was evident that God was with *him*, and therefor̄ till with them. He was high in station, the king's most trusted counsellor, yet he had never wavered in his loyalty to the faith of his fathers. His presence at Court was to them a strong consolation, for they knew how firmly with his keen prophetic vision he believed in the restoration of their national life.

According to the united showing of the prophets, therefore, hope might yet beat high in Jewish hearts. Their noblest possession was not lost. Let them lament over their long record of sin and folly, but let them not suppose that any earthly revolution could ever destroy the eternal spiritual truth of which the lost forms were only the temporary expression. There were promises of grace behind the judgment (Isa. xl. 2). With such men as these great prophets to advise them, live for them, and die for them, there was necessarily a future before the exiles as the people of God.

And what was the prophetic message to the heathen? *That*

---

[1] While it cannot, of course, be affirmed that the oracle against Babylon (Isa. xiii.–xiv. 23) is from the pen of the author of chaps. xl.–lxvi., there are strong reasons for regarding its date as *exilic*. Cf. G. A. Smith's *Isaiah*, i. p. 403; and Driver's *Isaiah*, pp. 85, 126, as well as his *Introduction to the Literature of the O.T.*

their idols were vanities, and that Jehovah was rightful Lord and Judge of all the earth. The prophets' mission to the Babylonians was to show the difference between Jehovah and their gods, and to cause the light of divine truth to shine forth in the stronghold of heathen divination. The soothsayers of Chaldea had occasion to measure their strength against the word of the Most High, and, needless to say, they signally failed in the unequal contest. As before in Egypt, so now in Babylon, confusion covered the gods of the land. What were they but powerless nonentities laboriously manufactured by their worshippers? (Isa. xl. 19, 20). What was the might of Babylon and of all other world-powers put together when thrown into the scale with the omnipotence of Jehovah? Rightly reckoned, it was but as the small dust of the balance (Isa. xl. 15). The Gentiles were to be taught where to look for the revelation of the will of the Supreme, who alone controls the destiny of nations, and to whom alone therefore are known the things of the future. Daniel, who was versed in all the wisdom of the Chaldees, did special service here. He was the brilliant and consistent representative to the idolaters on the plain of Dura of a wisdom that exceeded theirs as far as the heavens are higher than the earth. This bold advocacy of the claims of Jehovah as the Supreme God not only exposed Daniel to the envy and hostility of the wise men of Chaldea, but also helped to bring down upon the Hebrew nation—of which he was the greatest living ornament—the virulent hatred of their heathen oppressors. Pious men who dared to publish a word of hope to their enslaved brethren were obliged to have recourse to anonymity, and even thus many of them probably died a martyr's death.

CHAPTER IV

THE RETURN FROM EXILE

The crash of Babylon's fall resounded throughout the Eastern world (Jer. l. 46). The long-looked-for tidings, "Babylon is fallen, is fallen," had at length reached the ears of the captive Israelites, and both they and the Chaldeans had now to call Cyrus lord. In this Persian prince they had as humane and generous a ruler as ever sat upon a throne. The Israelites especially received the most considerate treatment at his hands, and were preferred before their former rulers, who had to "take the millstones and grind." The change of dynasty did not affect the position of Daniel, who wore his honours as aforetime, and hailed the advent of Cyrus, of whom Jehovah had said, "He shall build My city, and let My captives go." It was this that made the Persian monarch of so much consequence to Daniel and his nation.

1. **The Decree of Liberation.**—When would freedom's morning dawn? As the time appointed for the Return drew near, this question continued to exercise increasingly the mind of the aged prophet who was bearing the burden of his nation, and than whom there is no grander figure in history. How often had he, "the typical Jew of his day," who spent his life amid the splendours of an Eastern Court, shut himself up in his chamber, laid aside his purple robe, and "with fasting, and sackcloth, and ashes," poured forth the prayer of penitence for himself and his fellow-countrymen before Him who turneth the hearts of princes whithersoever He will! With yearning eyes he looked ever upward and homeward; for as he prayed "the windows of his chamber were open towards Jerusalem." To him her very dust was dear. His noble self-sacrificing patriotism was now to have its reward. In all probability he had the satisfaction of drawing

up with his own hand the decree issued by Cyrus in the first year of his reign at Babylon, permitting and calling upon the exiled Jews to return to their own land. There can indeed be little doubt that, under God, Daniel was the means of persuading Cyrus to this magnanimous action. Jeremiah and Ezekiel had gone the way of all the earth ; but he was still spared to see how Jehovah would turn again the captivity of His people. And so at last the word was spoken that was to set Israel free. The language of Ezra i. 2, 3, would seem to indicate the correctness of the Jewish tradition that the prophecy of Isaiah—where he is mentioned by name—had been shown to Cyrus, and that this was what led him to publish the edict of restoration. Whatever may have been his motive, one thing is clear—he reversed the policy of the Assyrian and Babylonian kings, and permitted the exiles to leave the land where they had groaned beneath the yoke of the alien. God had fulfilled His promise : " I will say to the north, Give up ; and to the south, Keep not back ; bring my sons from far, and my daughters from the ends of the earth."

2. **The returning Remnant.**—The eagerness with which Daniel awaited the result may be imagined. He must have had his own fears ; for it could not have escaped his observation that life in Babylon had great attractions for many of his countrymen. In point of fact, multitudes of them elected to remain in the busy capital, where they could live in ease and opulence. They had no mind to go and help to clear away the rubbish from a barren rock, or to share the hardships awaiting the new settlers. Would not the neighbouring tribes annoy them with their petty hostilities ? Besides, what could a merchant do in Judea ? And for what were they asked to make such a sacrifice ? For a mere sentiment. So reasoned some among the exiles—exiles now, alas ! by choice. Others simply did not feel any interest in the proposed undertaking. They had intermarried with foreigners, and were virtually Babylonian citizens, no longer caring about Jewish genealogies. But there were also those who received the news

3

about the edict with enthusiastic delight. These were the faithful and pious souls who counted the wealth and pleasures of Babylon as nothing compared with the blissful prospect of dwelling once more in their own land. To see the walls of Jerusalem rise again, and the temple service restored, would more than compensate for every loss. In those who were thus minded lay the hope of Israel. Happily they had two good leaders—Zerubbabel, the hereditary prince of Judah, and Joshua, son of Jozadak and grandson of Seraiah, the last high priest who had officiated at Jerusalem. In the prime of life, and imbued with a spiritual earnestness equal to their social eminence, both were well fitted to serve their nation at this important juncture.

The number of Jewish exiles who proceeded to Palestine with Zerubbabel and Joshua was 42,360. Of these the great majority belonged to the tribe of Judah. Servants were not included in this enumeration, which is probably indeed confined to heads of households, in which case the full complement of persons who left Babylon must have been about 200,000. It is interesting to note the *personnel* of the returning remnant, all of whom had made good their title to rank as true Israelites. Out of the twenty-four courses of priests there went back but four;[1] and if this be an index to the choice of the exiles generally, it would imply that only *one-sixth* of them returned to Jerusalem. Yet these "sons of Aaron" had apparently retained more faith in the promises of God than the lower order of the Levites, of whom only seventy-four joined the patriotic band. Perhaps they were actuated by jealousy. In the plan of the new theocracy drawn up by Ezekiel, Jerusalem was to be the only place of sacrifice, and the sons of Zadok the only ministrants at the altar. The Levites were to be prohibited from exercising the priestly office, "because they ministered unto the house of Israel before their idols," and were to be practically servants to the Zadokites. It is therefore easy to understand how the Return would be much more attract-

---

[1] These numbered between them, however, more than 4000 priests (Ezra ii. 36-39).

ive to the priestly caste than to the Levitical. One other inference may be drawn from the figures given in Ezra : it was not the men of princely fortune who went back to settle in Judea. Among the whole company there were but 736 horses, 245 mules, 435 camels, and 6720 asses. Had they been rich people as a rule, their beasts of burden would have been more numerous. But it was better to have held fast their faith throughout those years of exile than to be increased with goods. No doubt some remained without apostatising from their religion ; and these did great service in keeping alive the worship of Jehovah. In after years, when the apostles went forth everywhere to preach the gospel, they could appeal with special power to these brethren of the Dispersion.

What an interesting sight it must have been to see the Jews leaving Babylon ! Chiefs and priests, Levites and people, singers and servants, went forth in joyous procession, inspired by the feeling that they were the children of God. Had they not, every one of them, proved their Jewish lineage, as well as their unquestionable devotion? Gradually, to the sound of trumpets, and with singing, they filed through the eastern gate. The days of their exile were ended. The ransomed of the Lord were returning to Zion with songs and everlasting joy upon their heads. Both the sorrows of exile and the joy of restoration are reflected in the literature of the period. The shout of gladness succeeded to the dirge of woe. They had a long and arduous journey before them, a second pilgrimage through the wilderness, but they viewed it as a march of victory. In the year B.C. 538 the exiles turned their backs on Babylon. Daniel remained behind. His heart was with them, but he felt that for their sakes he must still abide in the king's court, and await his death in the land where he had spent his life. After four or five months of toilsome journeying across 800 miles of desert, the pilgrims reached at length the shapeless ruins of the holy city.[1] The day of their

---

[1] "They travelled along what was afterwards called the royal road. It led them by the banks of the Tigris, past the mounds which marked the desolate

arrival was the day of Israel's resurrection ; on this day the name *Jew* was born.[1]

3. The Moral Effect of the Exile.—How thoroughgoing and valuable were the lessons they had learned in Babylon appears from the spirit of the restored remnant.   They had undergone a purifying process.   The evil heart of unbelief had been cast out of them, and their idolatrous propensities killed.   They had gone away steeped to the lips in corruption ; they came back a reverent and pious people.   Like many persons still, they had learned in adversity what nothing could impress upon them so long as they were in prosperity.   As Dante has said—

> " Here are the treasures tasted that with tears
>   Were in the Babylonian exile won,
>   When gold had failed them."[2]

The Israelites were now prepared, as they had never been before, to think of a *suffering* Messiah.   Their own acquaintance with grief was the illustration to their minds of the ideal servant of the Lord as the Man of Sorrows.   The whole prophetic picture of Jehovah's servant, "tried and glorified by sufferings," rests upon that experience of sorrow by which they themselves had been disciplined and purified.   Thus did the Exile prove to be rich in ethical and spiritual results.   A moral revolution had taken place in the character of the nation.   There was such a revival of spiritual life as is pointed to in Ezekiel's prophecy : " From all your filthiness and from all your idols will I cleanse you, . . .

site of Nineveh, and the ancient city of Haran, with its temple of the Moon-god, which had been recently half destroyed by barbarian invaders, to the ford over the Euphrates that had once been commanded by the Hittite capital Carchemish.   From thence the exiles must have turned to the south by the way of Aleppo and Hamath, and so at last have found themselves again in their own land."—Sayce, *Introd. to Ezra*, etc., p. 19.

[1] " That is the name they were called by from the day that they came up from Babylon."—Josephus, *Ant.* xi. 5. 7.   It arose, doubtless, from the pre-dominance of the tribe of Judah.

[2] *Paradise*, xxiii. 128–130.

and ye shall dwell in the land which I gave to your fathers; and ye shall be My people, and I will be your God." Those who had returned from Babylon now felt the force of the prophetic doctrine of the remnant, and realised that before that remnant there lay a glorious task. For this their bondage in a foreign land had fitted them by throwing them back completely on themselves. The loss of outward power and pomp had the effect of strengthening their inward life, and this gave them a far greater power than any temporal prosperity could bestow. How truly had Ezekiel declared there was some better thing than earthly glory! The arm of flesh had failed them; but now they began to have a new consciousness that the everlasting arms were underneath them. To the nation at large the blow of the Exile had seemed like death; the true saints of the time perceived it to be the resurrection to a new life.

BOOK II

THE PERSIAN PERIOD, B.C. 537–333

———✦———

CHAPTER I

THE JEWS UNDER CYRUS AND HIS SUCCESSORS

1. Cyrus the Deliverer.—The royal dynasty of Persia first attained world-wide eminence in the person of Cyrus the Achæmenian.[1] The accounts of his origin are very obscure. Scripture is silent, and the Greek historians are contradictory and unreliable. Herodotus had apparently to choose between different traditions; and in his *Cyropædia*, Xenophon romances. In the pages of these writers it is the ideal ruler rather than the actual Cyrus that is presented. Apart from the fact that he was related to the last of the Median kings, and served in some capacity at the Court of Astyages, the early years of Cyrus remain, so far as the historians are concerned, enveloped in myth. We are, however, no longer wholly dependent on these authors, who lived long after him, for information regarding his extraction, his achievements, his religious standpoint, and his political aims. This old-world monarch has now spoken to us himself. There came to our country, in 1850, a Babylonian brick, on which he declares himself to be "the son of Cambyses, king of nations." His princely descent is therefore established.

---

[1] Whether Achæmenes is to be regarded as a historical figure is uncertain.

This find has, however, been dwarfed by more recent discoveries. Two documents which have been brought to light disclose the real circumstances attending the collapse of Babylon, the entrance of Cyrus into the city, and his seizure of "the sceptre of the world." One of these, a tablet of clay, has preserved to us the annals of the reign of Nabonidus. The other is the famous Cylinder Inscription of Cyrus.[1] In this valuable literary relic, which is virtually a continuation of the history, he magnifies his own exploits, and calls himself the vicegerent of Bel-Merodach, the city's patron god.

It is as the conqueror of Media that Cyrus steps out into the arena of history. After the capture of the seven-walled Ecbatana, he found himself "the great king." In a year or two (B.C. 549–546) he had added Persia to his territory, the people being content to find in him one who was likely to lead them to the victorious possession of regions long coveted. Lydia, the realm of the wealthy Crœsus, and the Greek cities of Asia Minor, next came to own his sway. The conquest of Babylon left him the most powerful monarch in the world.

The results of the fresh light thrown upon the rise of the Persian power by the cuneiform writings are mainly these : (1) Cyrus was king of Elam before he was king of Persia, and therefore retained Susa as one of his capitals in preference to Persepolis.[2] This also explains the reference in Isa. xxi. 2 to Elam[3] and Media as the source of Babylon's downfall. (2)

---

[1] "The Cylinder of Cyrus is barrel-shaped, about 9 inches long, with a diameter of 3¼ inches at the end, and 4½ inches at the middle. It contained originally nearly one thousand words, in Babylonian cuneiform. Apparently it had been deposited by Cyrus among the archives of one of the great temples of Babylon, soon after his capture of the city. The Annalistic Tablet measures about 4 inches by 3½ inches, and originally contained two columns of writing on either side. Both cylinder and tablet are now in the British Museum."—Hunter, *After the Exile*, i. p. 2.

[2] The empire, now firmly established, could boast of three royal residences: Susa or Shushan (spring), Ecbatana (summer), and Babylon (winter).

[3] Elam is probably to be identified with Susiana, a rich province of Lower Mesopotamia, situated between the mountains of Iran and the Tigris. Its

Cyrus entered Babylon in peace. (3) Cyrus was not a disciple of Zoroaster, but a polytheist, prepared to recognise the gods worshipped by every section of his subjects.[1] To the Jews, indeed, he calls Jehovah "the God of heaven" (Ezra i. 2); but to the Babylonians he has another name for the Supreme—"Merodach my Lord." His religious policy, in fact, was like that of Frederick the Great, who, shortly after his accession to the throne of Prussia, gave forth these memorable words : "All religions must be tolerated, and the fiscal must have an eye that none of them make unjust encroachment on the other ; for in this country every man must get to heaven in his own way."[2]

The traditional opinion as to the character of Cyrus is well known. The historians are lavish in their praise, but they simply record the Persian estimate. The picture drawn by them is that of an upright and noble prince, under whose administration even the subjugated nations could live in happiness and prosperity. On any view Cyrus must rank high among great conquerors. The records given up by the dead past show, however, that his success in building up the vast empire which stretched from the Black Sea to the Persian Gulf was due more to the shrewdness of his policy than to any exceptional strength of moral or religious principle. Apparently he considered the deportation of vanquished peoples a mistake in policy, and bade the various nationalities that had been forcibly carried to Babylon betake themselves to the several quarters whence they came. This, of course, earned their gratitude and goodwill. It proved, moreover, that he was a wise prince, who knew human nature. For

population was originally Semitic (Gen. x. 22). It possessed a civilisation as old as that of Babylonia, which in the days of Abraham seems to have been in a measure subject to it (cf. the way in which Chedorlaomer king of Elam figures in Gen. xiv.). Elam was blest with a race of men who knew how to defend their country. They were clever archers (Jer. xlix. 35 ; Xenophon, *Cyrop.* ii. 1. 16).

[1] "May all the gods whom I have restored to their strong places daily intercede before Bel and Nebo, that they should grant me length of days."— *Cylinder of Cyrus.*

[2] Carlyle's *Frederick the Great,* iv. p. 11.

the rest, he generously rewarded those who served him well, and refused to stain his hands with the blood of his three great adversaries.

The real importance of Cyrus for Israelitish history lies in his decree permitting the Jews to return to Palestine and rebuild their temple. Those who availed themselves of the offer received also his hearty good wishes, his powerful protection, and a liberal provision for the work of building and for the sacrificial rites. The sacred vessels removed by Nebuchadnezzar he magnanimously restored, counting out every one to "the prince of Judah" prior to the departure of the caravan. There are diverse accounts of his death ; but all (except Xenophon) agree that, after having reigned for twenty-nine years, Cyrus fell in battle (B.C. 529). His body was rescued by the Persians, who buried him in his native quarter of Pasargadæ. Near the ruins of Persepolis his tomb is still pointed out, and some pillars bear the inscription : "I am Cyrus, the king, the Achæmenian."

A marvellous career, truly, was that of Cyrus ; but it is fully accounted for by the simple explanation that he was "Jehovah's Shepherd," of whom it had been said : "He shall perform all My pleasure" (Isa. xliv. 28). The prophet assured the Jewish people that there was nothing degrading about the way by which liberty had come to them. That Cyrus was a foreigner simply showed that Jehovah could gather His weapons from any quarter He chose. The appearance of the mighty Persian was like a star of hope to the Jews. Under his reign matters became much brighter for them, although they soon discovered that their forecast had been over-sanguine. They could not indeed connect him directly with the fulfilment of their Messianic hopes, which centred around One who was to arise out of their own nation ; but, short of this, what was there of good that they did not look for at the hands of "the righteous man from the East"?

2. Back to Jerusalem. Preparations for rebuilding the Temple. —The exiles seem to have reached Palestine in spring. All

were obliged to settle in the vicinity of the capital, with a view to
consolidation against the hostile elements around. During the
half century they had spent in Babylon their land had been
overrun by incomers from various quarters. Only by the express
authority of Cyrus had a space of little more than twenty miles
square been cleared for them. But even this narrow lodgment
was a welcome change from the indignities connected with
captivity. Restoration to Jerusalem meant possession of the
temple, and in their eyes this was more to be desired than the
world itself. It was their zeal for Jehovah's house that had made
them leave the fertile plains of Babylonia for a region which,
whatever it had once been, was now by comparison a barren
waste. The ravages of Nebuchadnezzar's armies had been
followed by the still greater ravages of Time. In such a hilly
district as that of Judea, where vines were grown on the terrace-
system still in vogue in the Rhine provinces, the degradation
arising from neglect must have been of a very rapid kind. In
spite, therefore, of the great hope by which they were inspired,
the prospects of a comfortable existence for these patriotic Jews
were manifestly remote. Everything was to do ; temple, city,
walls—all had to be built. Their first care was, of course, to get
themselves housed. Nor was this an easy matter, especially for
the dwellers in Jerusalem, which had become a mass of ruinous
heaps, and a jackals' den (Jer. ix. 11). Their next task was the
restoration of their ancestral worship. Only six months elapsed
before " the people gathered themselves together as one man to
Jerusalem " to begin the holy work. In haste they built the altar
of burnt-offering, so as to be free alike from any harassing
opposition or embarrassing offer of co-operation from the
" people of those countries." The site of Solomon's altar having
been discovered, a wise and tender regard for old and sacred
associations led them to set up the new one on the same spot.
They brought back no new religion from Babylon ; it was theirs
merely to restore. From the first day of the seventh month
(Tisri)—afterwards celebrated as New Year's Day—the sacrificial

service began to be regularly observed. It happened, too, to be the season of the Feast of Tabernacles, which was joyfully kept. The enthusiasm of the people, indeed, was such that they went on to restore as far as possible the religious year. But they felt sadly the need of a temple. Their relation to the Holy Land, the possession of the sacred vessels, and the presence of the priesthood as a revived order—all this painfully reminded them that they had as yet no "house of Jehovah." It was to their credit that they were too zealous to wait for a temple before instituting their sacrificial worship, but equally so that they were too devoted to remain content without a temple now that they had an altar. They were, besides, committed to this by the terms of their release from Babylon, and accordingly they began to make the needed preparations. Money flowed in ; there was plenty of stone to be had for the quarrying ; and as formerly, in the days of Solomon, rafts of cedars were floated from Lebanon to Joppa, the port of Jerusalem. Many of their own number had gained skill as masons and carpenters in Babylon, and wages were paid to these workmen out of the general building fund.

Seven months were spent in getting materials ready, so that spring had again come round when the foundations of the Second Temple were laid. This ceremony took place in the month Ijar (April), B.C. 536. It was a great event for the new community. In one sense it was the goal they had looked forward to ; but it was also the starting-point of their new life. An outburst of praise, like the shout of Xenophon's men on sighting the sea, accompanied this first instalment of their glorious task. The priests blew their trumpets, the sons of Asaph sounded their cymbals, the people "sang together by course." The choral service over, Zerubbabel proceeded to lay the foundation-stone, whereupon "all the people shouted with a great shout." Yet the feelings called forth by this event were of a mingled kind. While the younger generation shouted for joy, the aged, who remembered the glory of the former Zion, broke forth into weeping. It is a touching picture—an emblem of man's life and work, in which the sorrows of memory frequently contend with the pleasures of hope. The prevailing feeling, however, must have been that which found expression in the Psalm : "Thou shalt arise, and have mercy upon Zion : for the time to favour her, yea, the set time, is come."

3. The Feud with Samaria.—But trouble was in store for the Jewish patriots. The recent doings at Jerusalem had necessarily attracted the attention of the neighbouring tribes,[1] the "peoples of the land," and "adversaries of Judah and Benjamin." Although these are general terms, the history makes it clear that the reference is to the singular composite race who for five and twenty centuries have borne the despised and distinctive name of "Samaritans." They formed the new population arising from the union of the settlers drafted in from Assyria with the portion of Israel still remanent after the deportation of the ten tribes. The facts as to their origin afford the best clue to the religious life of the earlier Samaritans. Theirs was by no means a pure worship, but a syncretistic compound ; and the foreign cults seem to have at first overshadowed the worship of Jehovah. Possibly the stricter Jews had been from the beginning offended at this jumbling together of Jehovahism and paganism, and had kept themselves aloof from these Samaritans ; but there are no distinct traces of this before the Exile. In Josiah's time the state of matters in the northern sanctuaries was very much what it had been during the prophetic activity of Amos and Hosea ; and there is evidence to show that the royal reformer had succeeded in keeping many of the Samaritan people in touch with the temple-service at Jerusalem (Jer. xli. 5). It was upon the Return that there was brought about the fierce estrangement expressed in the proverb : "The Jews have no dealings with the Samaritans."

Soon after the laying of the foundation-stone, the Samaritans requested to be allowed, as worshippers of the same God ever

---

[1] The Septuagint says : "They came to find out what was meant by the sounding of the trumpets," ὁ Ἰησοῦς v. 63.

since Esarhaddon had settled them there, to join in the national work of rebuilding the temple. There is no reason for doubting the good faith of this approach. It was probably made at the instance of the nobler part of the community, who, in their struggle against the polytheistic tendencies that continued to influence their public life, perceived what benefit would accrue to them from union with the fountain-head of the ancient faith. Thus early, at all events, did the affairs of the new colonists reach a crisis. They had now to settle once for all their attitude towards outsiders; for this was the larger question raised by the offer that had been made. It soon transpired that the great body of the people, instead of being prepared to welcome the outside world, desired to keep themselves hermetically sealed against it. They had suffered enough from coquetting with heathen neighbours, and would not enter into relations with any community whose Hebrew faith and lineage were open to suspicion. They were determined to cling to the religious isolation learned and practised in Babylon; and undoubtedly there was a lofty *morale* in the spirit that dictated their choice. Zerubbabel and his co-adjutors cannot have been blind to either the fair side or the dark side of the Samaritan proposal. Wisely enough, however, they based their decision on grounds entirely political. They said they must keep to their bond: Cyrus had given them no power to combine with others for the purpose mentioned in the royal edict. So keenly did the Samaritans feel the rebuff, that they at once became the declared enemies of the Jews. The old animosities of North and South were kindled afresh. In several respects the Samaritans had a strong position, and they began to make their power felt. They resolved on a policy of malicious and· organised revenge, which was only too successful. By an opposition at once active, scheming, and persistent, carried on not only by terrorism in Palestine, but also by lying intrigues at the Court of Persia, they contrived to obstruct the progress of the building "all the days of Cyrus," and during the next two reigns as well. Not that the edict of Cyrus was cancelled, but the mere fact that inquiries had to be made delayed matters indefinitely. Busied with the affairs of a vast kingdom, the Persian monarch could not give his attention to an insignificant community like that of Jerusalem.   And so the poison of calumny proved effectual in spite of all that Daniel and other Jewish friends at Court could do.   It was not until the second year of Darius Hystaspis that any real progress was made.   The people's hearts began to sink under the weight of difficulties for which they were not prepared.   They had put too much "confidence in princes" (Ps. cxviii. 9).

4. **The Successors of Cyrus.**—Cyrus was succeeded in the year 529 by his son Cambyses, whom he had already installed as "King of Babylon."   The one ambition of Cambyses was the subjugation of Egypt, and towards this end immense military preparations were made.   He began a dark career by secretly murdering Bardes, his younger brother, lest he should endeavour to supplant him.   After this foul deed, which was soon to bring its own nemesis, he made, in 527, his contemplated invasion of Egypt.   This was so successful that, after the battle of Pelusium and the siege of Memphis, the country of the Pharaohs became a Persian province.   Cambyses remained for some time in Egypt, intending to make it a base for further conquests.   But fortune favoured him no more.   Offended at the treatment which his ambassadors, who were really spies, received at the hands of the Ethiopian king, he madly ordered his army to march, regardless of the fact that they were altogether unequipped for such an expedition.   One contingent of his troops, caught in a simoom, perished in the desert ; and with the other he was forced to retreat, owing to the failure of supplies.   On his return to Memphis there was great rejoicing over the birth of an Apis, or peculiarly marked bull-calf, regarded by the Egyptians as divine. Interpreting the general mirth as a public gloating over his misfortunes, Cambyses is said to have dealt the sacred beast a mortal wound, thereby giving deep offence to the whole native

population. According to the Greek authors, his occupation of Egypt was characterised by horrible and sacrilegious outrages. It is alleged that priests, temples, and even the resting-places of the dead, suffered at his desecrating hands. Herodotus, indeed, records it as his conviction that "by a great variety of proof, Cambyses was stark mad." Much of this "proof," however, the Apis story included, would seem to be fabulous. If not insane, he was certainly dissolute, brutal, passionate, despotic. His reign was a short one. A pretender, Gaumata by name, and a Magian, having in 522 personated his younger brother and usurped the government, the miserable king, while returning homeward to assert his supremacy, was deserted by his soldiers, and in his despair committed suicide. The false Bardes now ruled without a rival. He seems to have enjoyed considerable popularity—due perhaps to the announcement that for three years no one would be asked to pay taxes or serve in the army. His supremacy had lasted only seven months, when by a conspiracy of the leading Persian families, who knew him to be an impostor, he was done to death in a Median fortress (B.C. 521).

Of the condition of the colony in Judea during those eight years we have no chronicle, but Jewish tradition represents them as having been extremely calamitous. Persian armies, with recruits probably from Edom and Samaria, would frequently be passing through Palestine, and this must have pressed sorely on the Jews. Nothing is known of the relations between them and these Persian monarchs beyond what is implied in the general statement that the temple-building ceased until the reign of Darius.[1] From this we may infer that these kings continued the policy of obstruction. There could indeed be little doubt that as a Magian who would have nothing to do with temples at all, and

---

[1] Josephus refers to this period the narrative in Ezra iv. 6-23, and in this is followed by Ewald and others, who identify Ahasuerus with Cambyses, and Artaxerxes with Bardes. But elsewhere in Scripture Ahasuerus is Xerxes, and it is therefore most natural to suppose that the section iv. 6-23 is episodic, and that the events it records really belong to the reigns of Xerxes and Artaxerxes I.

who razed to the ground the Persian temples of Ormazd, Bardes would be ready enough to oblige the Samaritans by placing an interdict upon the operations at Jerusalem. His own lease of power, however, was a very brief one ; and his death was the occasion of the dawn of fresh hope to the Jewish settlers.

CHAPTER II

THE JEWS UNDER DARIUS

1. Accession and Government of Darius.—One of the conspirators against Bardes, Darius Hystaspis, was the next monarch. He began to reign B.C. 522. A scion of the ancient house that produced the founder of the empire, his name rivals that of Cyrus himself. In his Great Inscription on the rock of Behistun, graven in the Elamite, Persian, and Chaldean tongues, he says : "Eight kings of my race have held the kingdom before me : in two lines [1] we have been kings." Darius proclaimed himself the true successor of Cyrus ; but as a Persian and a disciple of Zoroaster his sovereignty was unwelcome to many of the nationalities whom that monarch had subdued. Cyrus had been so versatile and accommodating in his religious views, that they had felt it to be no indignity to be his subjects ; but with Darius it was otherwise. They rightly anticipated that if *he* was to be head of the empire, the influence of Persia would be supreme, and Zoroastrianism the religion of the State. For some years, therefore, his tenure of the throne was insecure. In Susiana, Babylon,[2] Armenia, Arachosia, and even in Persis,

---

[1] Those, viz., of Elam and Persia.

[2] At this time probably occurred the protracted siege of Babylon referred to by Herodotus, and in connection with which the otherwise unknown "Darius the Mede" figures in the Book of Daniel.

serious troubles arose. Claimants, really or professedly descended from old and royal lines, were in some cases actually crowned as kings. Darius was, however, a man of extraordinary vigour and decision, and contrived to unify the empire so that he "reigned from India even unto Ethiopia," as did his son after him. His next care was to introduce a detailed system of government; and in this he succeeded so well that the institutions of Persia became henceforth monuments to his genius. His government, which was despotic, had its headquarters at the new capital of Susa, where the main roads converged. Dividing his empire into nearly thirty provinces, Darius appointed over each a governor or "satrap," who was held bound to raise and send into the imperial exchequer a certain fixed yearly tribute, and to maintain law and order within the sphere of his jurisdiction. By employing them as satraps he restored the prestige of the Persian nobles, who had been harshly treated under Bardes. For most of the provinces there was a separate military officer, and in all of them were located royal secretaries like Rehum (Ezra iv.), whose duty it was to transmit annually to the king a report upon the conduct of the satrap. An efficient system of roads, bridges, and posting stations was maintained out of the national funds. The tribute-money also sufficed to enable Darius to issue a coinage famed for its purity. His gold darics exceeded by about $\frac{1}{10}$th the value of an English sovereign. To the gross revenue of four or five millions sterling, Persia itself contributed nothing. The Indian province yielded the largest amount, and Babylon the next. Syria was one of the smaller satrapies, and included the district of Judea, which was managed by a *pekhah*, or officer under the satrap. Like the Roman governors in later times, these men were often guilty of extortion. The Jews knew this to their cost after Zerubbabel had passed away. During the reign of Darius, whose religious creed sufficiently resembled theirs to incline him to be sympathetic, their lot seems to have been a tolerably happy one. So long as they paid their taxes (Neh. v. 4), which were not oppressive, and provided the stipulated

4

number of army recruits (Neh. ix. 37), they had perfect liberty both social and religious.

2. Apathy of the Jews.—But their first experiences in Palestine had been peculiarly trying. Ever since the check sustained while Cyrus yet reigned, the building of the temple had been at a stand-still. The word "anarchy" might be written across the twelve years that had intervened. In consequence, the Jews had been largely at the mercy of unfriendly neighbours. Their crops, too, had failed, so that their condition must have been truly miserable (cf. Zech. viii. 10). A selfish spirit began to infect the community. They cared more to provide themselves with cieled houses than for the restoration of the house of Jehovah (Hag. i. 2-4), and easily persuaded themselves that it was not a suitable time for the latter work. The blight of apathy had fallen upon the people, and withered up their holier instincts. They had lost heart. Instead of watching for an opportunity of resuming their task, they settled down into lazy acquiescence. A year and a half had now passed since the accession of Darius without an effort being made. Even the zeal of their leaders would seem to have become dormant. Their hands had been "made idle," not merely by the opposition of their adversaries, but by the sluggishness of their own hearts. It is when enthusiasm is low that resistance becomes formidable. The gain of the new settlers amounted simply to this, that they had once more got a footing in their own land. For the rest, they had but exchanged the yoke of Babylon for that of Persia. Not yet, it would seem, was Jehovah propitiated towards them, not yet could they hail the arrival of the predicted Messianic days.

3. Haggai and Zechariah.—The little community was shaken out of its torpor by the powerful instrumentality of a prophetic voice. The crisis was such as to call for divine interference. If the temple possessed the highest significance for the kingdom of God in its Old Testament form, this was more than ever the case now that the Jews had practically ceased to be a nation, and had become a religious sect. The rebuilding of it was the presupposition of the renewal of covenant fellowship. So long, therefore, as they permitted it to lie waste, they were shutting themselves off from the fulfilment of the divine promises. This had been felt all along by the minority among the Jews—the party of progress ; but now they found a spokesman in the prophet Haggai. Although nothing is known as to the circumstances of his life, it is probable that he was old enough to remember Jehovah's house in its first glory (ii. 3). It was in the sixth month of the second year of Darius (B.C. 520) that this venerable figure appeared before the national leaders as "the Lord's messenger in the Lord's message." Not for sixteen years had the voice of prophecy been heard, but it had lost none of its ancient power. In some respects, indeed, there is a marked contrast between Haggai and the great prophet of the Exile. There is no lofty idealism in his utterances. His range is narrowed to the one consideration of building the temple, which in post-Exilic days acquired a new significance as the visible centre of Israel's worship. So long as it lies waste, they and their offerings are alike unclean in His sight (ii. 14). This prophet's language, too, is very homely and unadorned ; he is pre-eminently a practical preacher. His lively and interrogative periods, addressed in turn to people, prince, and priest, demand an answer at once. With unsparing severity he rebukes the inclination of many to enter into nice calculations as to whether the "seventy years" have yet run their course. He implores them to consider not their hindrances, but their ways, and assures them that if they build the temple the Lord will take pleasure in it (i. 8). A month later he asks them not to allow any comparison between the magnificence of the former temple and the poverty of their own to slacken their zeal. The silver and the gold are the Lord's. He will destroy the kingdoms of the heathen, and out of their treasures so beautify this latter house that its glory shall exceed even that built by Solomon (ii. 17). Once more, using an illustration from the priestly ritual, he alleges that they have only to proceed with the erection of the temple to be free from the pressure of famine, and to win the blessing of God (ii. 10–19). The experiences of the Exile had taught the danger of disregarding a prophetic oracle, and the response was immediate. Jehovah so "stirred up the spirit" of both leaders and people, that within three weeks from the day of Haggai's first remonstrance the work of restoration was being briskly carried forward (i. 15).

The spirit of enthusiasm was still further aroused, when two months later one of the younger men, Zechariah the son of Berechiah, the son of Iddo, upon whom the prophetic mantle had also fallen, joined with Haggai in urging the prosecution of the sacred task. Both prophets had essentially the same message ; their theme was repentance. They declared that there was no justification for delay. Nor indeed was there. Although the hostility of the neighbouring tribes had hitherto prevented it from being carried out, the decree of Cyrus had never been revoked. The Jews were therefore still at liberty to proceed. But the two prophets based their exhortations upon a far higher ground—that of duty. Apart from the erection of the temple, the new colony must prove a failure. Let them penitently abandon their ungodly sloth, and address themselves with diligence to this work. Such was Heaven's "categorical imperative" for them. Zechariah, who belonged to the priestly aristocracy, and whose prophecies date from Marchesvan (October), B.C. 520, to Chisleu (November) 518, proved a valuable coadjutor to Haggai. He quite overshadows his older fellow-prophet, and is altogether a man of larger mould. At once he saw the peculiar canker that was eating the heart out of the popular effort to re-establish on a proper footing the worship of Jehovah, and with characteristic force set himself to uproot it. What seemed likeliest to wreck the good enterprise was the disposition of many to dwell upon the glories of the past in such a way as to dishearten the workers of the present. With this tendency, which is to some extent inherent in human nature,[1] Zechariah had no patience. To his thinking there was not much

---

[1] Compare the way in which Horace satirises the "laudator temporis acti se puero."—*Ars Poetica*, 173.

that was ideal about Israel's past. If there was one word more than another which he wished to address to his hearers, it was this : " Be ye not as your fathers " (i. 4). Who had brought all these calamities upon them ? Their fathers, who had been appealed to again and again to abandon their evil ways, and would not. Let them therefore refrain from this false glorification of a bygone age ; let the past history of their nation be their warning rather than their pride.

4. Interference of Persian Officials: continued Influence of the Prophets: Edict of Darius.—Under this prophetic stimulus the work of rebuilding went forward by leaps and bounds. The breath of opposition did not, however, cease to blow. The Persian officials, prompted by the Samaritans, or by their own sense of duty, demanded to know by what authority and by what persons the work was being carried on. As the Jews took high ground, asserting themselves to be " the servants of the God of heaven," and fell back on the decree of Cyrus as their political justification, Tatnai could do nothing until " the matter came to Darius." In his reference of the question to the Great King he suggested that a search should be made among the official records of Babylon, so as to test the accuracy of the Jewish contention. Meanwhile, "as though God's eye protected them," and with His prophets at their back, the people prosecuted their arduous task. Still they could not forget that everything depended on the outcome of the official report. What if the record bearing that Zerubbabel was the emissary of Cyrus were lost ? On the 24th of the ninth month, Haggai once more exhorted the people, and assured Zerubbabel that amid the upheaval of thrones and kingdoms that would precede the glorious establishment of God's house, his would be a position of absolute security, seeing he was the chosen servant of the Almighty, precious to Him as His signet ring. Although the story narrated in the apocryphal book of 1 Esdras is unhistorical, it is not unlikely that at this stage Zerubbabel visited in person the Court of Darius, with the view of checkmating the influences there.

Nor would the home interests of the Jews thereby suffer. They had in Zechariah one who could more than fill the place of their absent leader. In any case this prophet now came to the front. With the tongue of the learned, and the voice of authority, he knew how to speak the seasonable word to a people weary with disappointment, and much in need of wise guidance. On the 24th of the eleventh month (January), Zechariah, in language glowing with Eastern imagery, exhorted the people to exercise patience, to look at their growing city, to confide in their leaders, to expect the expulsion of evil-doers, to look for a happy ending to all their distresses, and for perfect immunity from oppression on the part of such powers as Egypt and Babylonia. It was a mistake to despise the day of small things. Not by might nor by power did success come, but by the Spirit of the Lord. The foundation of the house had been laid by Zerubbabel ; his hands would also finish it (iv. 7-10). The prophet closed his address with the remark that the Spirit of the Lord was resting on the north country (vi. 8) ; and indeed—as appears from the appendix, vi. 9-15—the sympathetic attitude of the Babylonian Jews soon showed itself in the arrival of three deputies with gifts for the temple. These wealthy brethren of the Dispersion had been rather tardy with their help. Haggai had already indicated a coming change in this respect (ii. 7) ; and Zechariah pointed to the offerings conveyed by these sons of the captivity as evidence that at last the flowing tide was with the patriotic dwellers of Jerusalem. Many of their kindred " from afar would come and build in Jehovah's temple " (vi. 15). Meanwhile the prophet must make out of the precious metals transmitted from Babylon a crown for Joshua the high priest. It is significant that the prophet, while predicting the speedy completion of the temple, says nothing about the restoration of the monarchy. Probably he wanted to indicate that, even in the absence of a king, Israel had in the high priest a foreshadowing of the Messiah. In chap. vi. 12, 13, Zechariah places ruler and priest—"the two anointed ones " (iv. 14)—upon a level, with a forward look to the combination of both offices in the person of "The Branch," the true Builder of Jehovah's temple. After it had served its purpose in calling attention to this, the coronet which had been placed on Joshua's head was to grace the new temple, and be to future generations a memorial of an act of piety that deserved to become historic. While it should glitter on the sacred walls, the three bearers of the offering—Helem, Tobijah, and Jedaiah—and their worthy host, Josiah, would never cease to be held in honour; so often as the worshipper's eye should light upon it, he would rejoice in it as a symbol of Israel's unity.

That the prophets, in urging on the work of building despite the challenge of the Persian governor, did not buoy up either people or leaders with a false hope, the event soon showed. At Babylon, indeed, the necessary document was not found; but there existed in the library at Ecbatana, along with similar State papers, a "roll" with a copy of the edict of Cyrus. The decision therefore was in favour of the Jews. The government officials were instructed to "let the work of the house of God alone." Darius, in a new decree, even required them to supply funds for building and materials for sacrifice, and that daily as the priests might appoint, penalties, both civil and religious, being enacted in the event of non-compliance with the statutory provisions.

5. Completion and Dedication of the Temple: its Inferiority to the First.—In the sixth year of Darius, B.C. 516, on the 3rd Adar (February), twenty-one years after the laying of the foundation, the headstone of the temple was brought forth with shoutings, and the people cried, "Grace, grace unto it!" (Ezra vi. 15; Zech. iv. 7). As in the case of Solomon's temple, the event was celebrated by the keeping of a solemn festival. It was impossible for Zerubbabel to vie with the magnificence of Israel's most prosperous monarch, and of her palmiest days; but what could be done was done. A comparison of Ezra vi. 17 with 1 Kings viii. 63 shows that on this occasion the sacrifices were in the proportion of only one to two hundred; yet, if they were few in number, they were, at all events, accompanied by that humble confession of sin, without which the greatest plethora of sacrifices would have been unacceptable. The feeling of national unity found fitting expression in the offering of "twelve he-goats" as a sin-offering for all the tribes of Israel. They looked upon the temple as their common possession. As before the sorrows of exile and the trials of the restoration-time, so now the success of their enterprise welded them into one. The peculiar gladness that is felt after sorrow made this the occasion of a joy more intense even than that called forth by the dedication of the first house.[1]

From this date also the public service of God began to be carefully ordered. "The priests were set in their divisions, and the Levites in their courses." No time was lost in using the completed building, for this after all was the true consecration. The Passover was observed on the 14th of Nisan, the first month of the new year (March, B.C. 515). Not since the days of Josiah had this feast been kept, so that one more was added to the list of memorable Passovers. The sacred observance was shared in by "all such as had separated themselves from the filthiness of the heathen of the land." "Jehovah had made them joyful"; He had touched the heart of the Assyrian king, and had gathered together these outcasts of Israel. Surely these were signs that He was building up Jerusalem (Ezra vi. 21, 22 ; Ps. cxlvii. 2).

We have little detailed information regarding this second temple. According to Ezra vi. 3, 4, it had a height and breadth of sixty cubits, and was surrounded by three storeys of chambers. This apparently exaggerated estimate—it throws the Solomonic temple into the shade—is probably reached by reckoning the height from the door of the outer court to the pinnacle, and the breadth as between the outer walls. But it is also possible that Cyrus may have designed a larger edifice than Zerubbabel was able to build. The new structure stood upon the site of the earlier one, which it probably resembled in plan as well. Several courts and chambers, porches and vestibules, were attached to it

[1] Cf. Luke xv. 32.

(1 Macc. iv. 38, 48). Josephus mentions that there were galleries in the porches, and that at the time of Pompey a bridge connected it with the city on the north-west side. There seems to have been ample accommodation for the priests and for the sacred vessels used in the Jewish ritual (Ezra x. 6 ; Neh. xiii. 5). Hecateus of Abdera says that no trees were planted within the precincts—a very obvious precaution against idolatry. Other distinctive features about the temple were the Court of the Gentiles ; the fortress (Bira) on the north side ; and the Eastern Gate, designated the Beautiful Gate (Acts iii. 2), or the Gate of Shushan, owing to its being adorned with a representation in sculpture of that Persian palace.

The Jews never looked upon the new building as equal to the temple of Solomon. Its inferiority lay not so much in size, however, as in grandeur. The gorgeous drapery, the exquisite carved work, the abundance of gold and silver plate, which were the glory of the first temple, were beyond the reach of the new settlers. A period of prosperity might go far to remedy this ; but there were other things precious in the eyes of the pious Jew which were absent from this temple, and which could never be regained. They had their altar once more ; they had " the candlestick of light and the table of the shewbread" (1 Macc. i. 21, 22) ; and on the day of atonement the high priest in his official robes again entered the Holy of Holies to sprinkle the sacrificial blood. But the Urim and Thummim no longer adorned the high priest's breastplate ; and there was a sad blank in the Holy of Holies.[1] The ark of the covenant was gone ; it had been burnt at the destruction of Jerusalem. The cherubim and the shechinah no longer visibly symbolised the presence of Jehovah. The tables of stone and the pot of manna, Aaron's rod and the golden shields, had all disappeared. This was certainly not an unmixed loss, in view of the more spiritual worship

---

[1] "In the Holy of Holies there was nothing at all."—Josephus (*De Bell. Jud.* v. 5. 5). " Nulla intus deûm effigie vacuam sedem et inania arcana" is the description of Tacitus (*Hist.* v. 9).

towards which God was gradually leading His people.   One other feature of the second temple must be noticed : it was much more of a priestly institution than the first.[1]   The laity were railed off from a part of the inner court altogether ; and pervading the whole ritual was the idea of the mediation of the priests.

6. The People's Lack of Spirit: their Meagre Territory.—The joy manifested at the dedication of the temple was apparently but a fitful gleam.   In the fourth year of Darius, Sharezer and Regem-melech, the authorities at Bethel,[2] sent deputies to consult the priests and prophets in Jerusalem as to the propriety of keeping up the fast days instituted during the Exile (Zech. vii. 2, 3).   Zechariah promptly declared that their fasts had never been of much value, and that in the sight of God the important things were truth, mercy, and righteousness.   It was not the presence of the temple, but the possession of these qualities by the people, that would make Palestine the Holy Land.   Instead, therefore, of defending the old days of mourning, the prophet recommended "joy and gladness and cheerful feasts" as better befitting the altered circumstances.   Brighter days, he said, were in store for Jerusalem.   The general happiness of the inhabitants would be betokened by the arrival of many at a serene old age, and by the mirthful gambols of boys and girls in the streets (viii. 4, 5).   The triumph of the divine kingdom also would be seen in the coming of many nations to seek and pray before the Lord ; people of every tongue would yet come under the spell of the Jewish faith (viii. 20–23).   The tendency to keep up the days of mourning outlived, however, the check it thus received.   Wor-

---

[1] "The first temple was primarily the royal chapel, and the kings did as they pleased in it ; the second temple was the sanctuary of the priests, whose chief now became the temporal as well as the spiritual head of the people."— W. Robertson Smith, article "Temple" in *Encyclopædia Britannica*.

[2] Zech. vii. 2.   Compare the marginal reading of the Revised Version, and C. H. H. Wright, *Zechariah and his Prophecies*, p. 166.

shipping their great past and dreaming about their still greater future, combined to produce in the hearts of the majority an almost morbid dissatisfaction with their present condition.

This is not the spirit of which growth comes ; and as a matter of fact the new community continued to occupy a very limited territory. Even with the further accessions they received from Babylonia, and from the ranks of compatriots who had been left behind in Palestine, the reconstituted Jewish nation covered but a fraction o the ancient kingdom of Judah. Hemmed in on every side by their enemies—Philistines to the west, Samaritans to the north, and Edomites to the south—they were restricted to an area not exceeding that of an ordinary Scottish *shire*, until three or four centuries later, under John Hyrcanus, they acquired some fresh tracts of territory.

7. Zerubbabel, the last Prince of Judah.—The work of restoration was regarded as the prelude to the restoration in all its glory of the Davidic kingdom. But did this imply a return to the temporal sovereignty? This question will be best answered by a glance at the career of Zerubbabel, in whom the great dynasty of David, after lasting for more than five hundred years, came to an end. The son of Shealtiel, and the grandson of King Jeconiah, Zerubbabel was during the Exile the recognised head of the tribe of Judah. With the dew of his youth yet upon him, he had patriotically led forth from Babylon the flower of his nation. Prior to this, under the name of Sheshbazzar, he had probably been a faithful servant at Court. Cyrus appointed him *pasha* or *tirshatha* of Judea, and in this capacity he continued to bear sway under Darius. Zerubbabel was the last of his race who held a princely office. In Judea his descendants were simply private citizens, although among the Jews of the Diaspora the title "Chief of the Captivity" was applied to the leading member of this family for the time being. Great hopes centred on Zerubbabel. But to himself, as to others, it became increasingly manifest that the Davidic throne was not to be re-established in his person. The way in

which his name drops out of the history is in itself an evidence
that the temporal sovereignty was now an impossibility in Israel.
To not a few this was a bitter disappointment. It was felt that
Jehovah had again cast off His people (Ps. lxxxix. 38); and that
the suppression of the throne was inconsistent with the divine
promise (Ps. lxxxix. 49, cxxxii. 10). This, of course, was not
really so; but if even in the time of our Lord many had not
ceased to expect a temporal prince, we can understand the outlook of wistful regret that dictated such sentiments in the Persian
epoch. To those who longed for the appearance of the Great
Deliverer who was to arise from the stem of Jesse, Zerubbabel
was naturally an object of interest as being, if not the Saviour of
Israel, at least His forerunner. And certainly "the way of the
Lord" was prepared in no small degree through his instrumentality and work. The importance of his official position was,
however, greater than the force of his personal character.
Oftener than once the prophets had to rouse his flagging zeal;
and but for the stimulus thus supplied, it is probable that the
latter part of his work would never have been accomplished. It
was no doubt a difficult task that he had to perform. His status
as a Persian official consorted ill with his claims as heir to the
throne of David, and the ever-increasing power of the priesthood
must have made it hard to preserve "the peace of Jerusalem"
(Ps. cxxii. 6). Such a situation demanded exceptional tact and
strength of will, and Zerubbabel was not the man to cope with it.
Tradition says that he died in Babylon. Along with him there
disappear also from the scene his leading associates—Joshua the
high priest, and the prophets Haggai and Zechariah. At this
stage the curtain falls on the little colony at Jerusalem, and
when it rises again a new generation is disclosed to our
view.

8. **Subsequent Career, Death, and Character of Darius.**—The
Great King had succeeded in consolidating his empire. But it
was not possible for an Eastern prince to rest content with a

"scientific frontier." On the banks of the Indus and of the Danube (about B.C. 515) he sought to win fresh laurels. In the latter case, however, owing to the nature of the country and climate, he was obliged to retreat. Darius now resolved to measure his forces against Greece. About the year 500 the cities of Asia Minor had risen in rebellion, and ultimately the Ionians and Athenians came to their aid, but in vain. They were routed at Ephesus, at Salamis, and at Miletus. An attempt was subsequently made under Mardonius to conquer Greece itself; but, in spite of some preliminary successes, the Persians were completely vanquished on the storied field of Marathon by the Athenians and Platæans under Miltiades. This may, without extravagance, be described as a turning-point in the world's history. Darius died in B.C. 485 at the age of sixty-three, while his armies were quelling an insurrection in Egypt. His long and interesting reign was distinguished not only by exceptional successes in war, but by many wise acts of peaceful administration. He was essentially a man of deeds. Weak, perhaps, in stratagem, he was yet prompt and impetuous in action. His ways were simple compared with the magnificence of Cyrus ; his spirit, strong and robust as that of Cambyses was luxurious and weak. Brave and relentless, he could be trusted to keep his word. His usual mode of designating his enemies was to call them rebels and liars ; and he sedulously fostered the impression that no one had anything to fear from the Great King unless he "spoke lies."

CHAPTER III

THE JEWS UNDER XERXES AND ARTAXERXES

1. **The reign of Xerxes, B.C. 485-464.**—Darius was succeeded by his eldest son, Xerxes. The brief statement of Ezra iv. 6, com-

prises all that is known of the condition of the Jews in Palestine under this monarch ; indeed, it is the only scrap of information we possess for the fifty-eight years between the dedication of the temple and the arrival of Ezra in the seventh year of Artaxerxes. What, then, do we learn from it ? Simply that "the people of the land, in the beginning of the reign of Ahasuerus (Xerxes), wrote unto him an accusation against the inhabitants of Judah and Jerusalem." The grounds of this charge are not specified, but the effect of it was to put a damper upon the new settlers. They soon found that they had nothing to hope for from Xerxes, destroyer though he was of Babylon, their ancient foe (Isa. xlvi. 1) ; and during his reign they seem to have degenerated socially, morally, and religiously (Neh. v. 3, 7, 9). Endeavours have been made to fill up this blank in the history, but none of them are satisfactory. Some of the early Church Fathers look to this period for the fulfilment of certain predictions regarding the repulsion of hostile invaders by the Jews (Ezek. xxxviii.; Joel iii.; Mic. iv. 11). Ewald finds the circumstances of the time reflected in a group of eight psalms, to which he assigns this as "the true date." In vain do we look for side-lights from extra-canonical sources. Part of the fleet wherewith Xerxes unsuccessfully assailed Greece (B.C. 480) is said by Herodotus to have been forthcoming from the coasts of Palestine ; but the reference points rather to the Philistines than to the Jews. Josephus (c. Apion, i. 22) cites a Greek poet who mentions the *Solymi* as having assisted Xerxes, and assumes that this name is given to the Jews ; but the Solymi were Lycians, and it was not till long after that Jerusalem was known as Solyma.[1] Additional interest circles round Xerxes as the Ahasuerus of the Book of Esther, which introduces us to him in "Shushan the palace," where he had gathered his tributary princes, and "showed the riches of his glorious kingdom and the honour of his excellent majesty many days." This work, however, throws no light on the state of the Palestinian Jews. There is no reference in it to the temple, or to the struggles of the

---

[1] Abbreviated form of Hierosolyma.

colonists ; they are not within its horizon at all.   It is simply a
story of the Persian Court, written probably just after the close
of the Persian age, showing how a great danger to their foreign
brethren was averted, and telling of the inauguration of the Feast
of Purim to commemorate the deliverance.   In character, Xerxes
was a "loud" man.   No one ever walked more in a vain show
than he did.   His fondness for display was the visual image of a
weak and cowardly spirit.   "He was accustomed to act like a
spoilt child," which very likely he was.   Mothers like Atossa
do not produce great sons.   Professedly a monotheist, and a
worshipper of Ormazd, Xerxes destroyed the temple of Bel, the
headquarters of idolatry in Babylon.   In the twentieth year of
his reign he was assassinated by Artabanus, the captain of his
bodyguard.

2. Ezra the Scribe.—When, in B.C. 458, the Jewish colony
emerges once more from historic darkness, it bears the marks of
decided deterioration.   Eighty years had passed since, full of
hope, the exiles had returned from Babylon ; for the third
generation of their descendants the star of hope had nearly set.
The apparently revived interest of their kinsmen in foreign parts
had not been sustained ; offerings for the enrichment of the
temple had not poured in according to expectation.   The Persian
governors, too, laid on them grievous burdens (Neh. v. 15) ; and
with their neighbours they had long been at daggers drawn.   In
their straits they began to modify their exclusiveness towards
"the people of the land," even to the point of intermarriage with
them.   The first to take this step were the priests and Levites,
and their example was largely followed.   But foreign wives did
not come alone ; they brought with them a foreign spirit.   The
consequence was that laxity soon took the place of zeal in connection with the observances of the law.   The Jews of the
Dispersion were really better representatives of their religion
than those now living in Jerusalem ; and if they did not visit the
temple so often or contribute to it so richly as they might have

done, they at all events kept holy the Sabbath, and were filled
with reverence for the Mosaic law.

> "To Kerke the narre, from God more farre,
>   Has been an old sayd sawe."[1]

Reform was urgently needed; but where were the few who
desired it to look for the reformer? The instrument was being
providentially prepared in Babylon in the person of Ezra the
Scribe.

Ezra possessed many qualifications for his difficult task. His
priestly lineage through Seraiah was in itself no small advantage.
But even more serviceable to him were his acquirements as a
scribe or exponent of the Mosaic law. As a student, interpreter,
and copyist of the law he had no equal; "he was a ready scribe"
(Ezra vii. 6). It was not at every point that the old law could be
applied in the altered circumstances of the nation, and it would
fall to the discernment of Ezra to make plain its essential principles, and to see that these found due expression in the national
life and worship. The character and accomplishments of Ezra
had also given him influence at Court. He was in high favour
with Artaxerxes Longimanus, the son and successor of Xerxes.
It was in the early part of this king's reign that Ezra heard about
the prevailing defection in Judea. He took the matter before his
royal master, who despatched him on a mission of inquiry "con-
cerning Judah and Jerusalem." Artaxerxes was no doubt a mild
prince, "easy to be entreated"; but the sort of *carte blanche*
given to Ezra points to a religious motive. He had learned, if
not to worship Jehovah, to have at all events a superstitious
dread of Him (Ezra vii. 23). Perhaps Esther's influence may be
traceable here. Ezra's deep and earnest piety may be reckoned
as a further element of fitness for his mission. He was a consecrated man, a saint and a patriot who had "set his heart to
seek the law of Jehovah, and to do it, and to teach in Israel
statutes and judgments." In his view the state of matters at

---

[1] Spenser, *The Shepherd's Calendar* (July).

Jerusalem was most ominous for the future of Judaism. The temple was, after all, but a means to an end, viz. the observance of the law. To neglect the legal ordinances was simply to throw away their opportunity as a nation.

3. Decree of Artaxerxes: Second Return of the Jews under Ezra.

—Artaxerxes issued a decree allowing Ezra a free hand in his work "for Jerusalem's sake." Both men and means were placed at his disposal. Liberal provision was made for the adornment of the temple and for the sacrificial service, the priests and other officials being also exempted from payment of tribute. It was made plain that Ezra went on his mission as a plenipotentiary of the Persian Empire. His great object was, of course, to instruct the people in the law, and on that basis to reform their public life ; but with a view to this he had conferred upon him the fullest magisterial powers. Those who refused to submit to his jurisdiction he was authorised to visit with imprisonment, confiscation of property, banishment, or even death.

It was on the first of Nisan (March), in the seventh year of Artaxerxes, that, accompanied by a quota of sympathetic disciples, Ezra set out for Judea. He had found men of character and position—"chief men"—to organise the expedition in various parts of Babylonia, and bring forward their several companies to the place of meeting by "the river of Ahava," a district which has not been identified. Ezra drew up a complete list, according to their several families, of those who were prepared to share his fortunes ; and from this it appears that the Aaronic and Davidic houses were not unrepresented. Including the contingent who joined them a few days after the halt at Ahava, the entire strength of the emigrants was about 1800 men ; and if allowance be made for their wives and little ones, we must think of a gathering of something like 7000 souls. On reviewing his company, Ezra discovered that it included no Levites. Desiring, however, to take with him a thoroughly representative band of colonists, he ultimately induced 38 Levites and 220 Nethinim to cast in their

5

lot with him.   The only thing needed now was God's protection, and for this special supplication was made.   They had reason to be concerned for their safety.   At no time was the desert free from brigands, and least of all would it be without its dangers now that the Persian troops, under Megabyzus, had been drafted to put down a rebellion in Egypt.   Ezra might have had the usual military escort, but in view of his already professed reliance upon the divine "hand," he was "ashamed" to ask for it, and determined to illustrate on a grand scale the sufficiency of his principle of trust in the Unseen.   Freewill offerings for the temple having been given into the custody of twelve priests and twelve Levites, the new emigrants left Ahava on the 12th of the first month (Nisan), and arrived at Jerusalem in the beginning of the fifth (Ab).   After a sacrificial expression of thanksgiving for journeying mercies, they delivered their commissions to the Persian authorities, who then "furthered the people and the house of God."

4. Ezra's Reformation.—Ezra assumed at once the rôle of the reformer.   The people had been drifting into lawless fusion with the neighbouring tribes, and endangering the Jewish faith and nationality.   The discovery of the extent to which the evil had been carried filled Ezra with horror, shame, and bewilderment ; he "sat astonied until the evening sacrifice."   Then he rent his garments, fell on his knees, and acknowledged before God the trespass of his nation.   While yet he lay paralysed with sorrow, his friends had gathered around him, and gradually, as the hour of the evening oblation approached, all eyes were turned towards the unwonted spectacle.   Many were in tears, as one of the people, Shechaniah, whose own family was implicated, spoke by way of interpreting Ezra's action.   He proposed that the mixed marriages should be dissolved, and the strange wives and their children put away.   He urged Ezra, moreover, to strike while the iron was hot.   Ezra was not the man to hesitate.   Immediately he rose, and the people took an oath "that they should do according to this word." The stern scribe withdrew to one of the side chambers of the temple, and conferred with the leaders of the community as to the best means of giving effect to the decision arrived at. It was agreed to summon to Jerusalem on the 20th of the ninth month all the "children of the captivity." All came, and undertook to separate themselves from their foreign wives. Ezra boldly declared this to be God's pleasure, although the dismissal of the heathen women (and in some cases also of their children, Ezra x. 44) was scarcely in accordance with the precepts of the Mosaic law [1] (cf. Ex. xxi. 10; Deut. xxi. 15). It is surprising that so few dissented [2] from the proposal to appoint a standing committee, with Ezra as president, to deal with the mixed marriages in each district. This body began its work on the 1st of the tenth month, and by the beginning of the new year, to use the rather callous phrase of the chronicler, "they made an end with all the men that had taken strange wives." The names of such as had promised to put them away were officially published, the list including four of high-priestly rank, thirteen other priests, ten Levites, and eighty-six laymen belonging to ten separate families. With this catalogue the Book of Ezra abruptly ends, and there are no further accounts of his administration until after an interval of twelve years.

5. **Ezra's Unsuccessful Attempt to fortify Jerusalem.**—Some light is thrown, however, upon the state of matters at Jerusalem during this period by the episode related in Ezra iv. 7-23, which falls chronologically between the Books of Ezra and Nehemiah.

---

[1] "Owing to the wife's dependent state, marriage with women not Israelites could not in general be specially objected to: compare the law on marriage with virgins taken in war, Deut. xxi. 10-13 (even Moses himself had a Cushite as wife, Num. xii. 1); only marriage with Canaanite women was absolutely forbidden, Ex. xxxiv. 16; Deut. vii. 3."—Oehler, *Old Testament Theology*, i. p. 334. In taking this step Ezra already began the process of "hedging" the law.

[2] See Ezra x. 15, where for "were employed about" read "stood up against."

From this it appears that Ezra and his associates, on effecting their work of reformation, went on to fortify the city also. As a community devoted to the law, they wished to defend their temple, and to shut out the contaminating influences of a pagan world. The envious opposition of their vigilant adversaries was soon excited, and letters of complaint were sent to the Persian Court. One was written in Aramaic, apparently by the satrap of Syria ; and another, the contents of which have been preserved, was despatched on behalf of the nationalities inhabiting the province of Samaria by " Rehum the lord of official intelligence, and Shimshai his secretary."[1] Their appeal was directed to the self-interest of the monarch, and was entirely successful. A search among the records, which bore that the city had, as alleged, a bad repute for insurrection, coupled with the fact that at the time he had his difficulties with Egypt, led Artaxerxes to veto the building operations at Jerusalem. For Ezra and his sympathisers the outlook must have been of the gloomiest. A deadly blow had been struck at the prestige and authority of the Great Scribe. His position was that of a statesman driven from office ; he had to possess his soul in patience while witnessing the reversal of his policy and the undoing of his work. The course of events had proved unfavourable. Megabyzus, the satrap of Syria, had quarrelled with the Court of Persia ; and Artaxerxes, after some years of warfare, was obliged to negotiate for peace. No Persian monarch had hitherto shown such weakness in dealing with a subject prince, and this fact may help us to understand the turn things had taken in Judea. The royal support was no longer worth what it had

---

[1] Ewald takes a peculiar view of Ezra iv. 6-23. Apart from his declinature to consider it as parenthetical, he regards the letter alluded to in ver. 7 as having been friendly to the Jews, and written by some of their own leading men in order to commend their newly-settled nation to King Artaxerxes. In this case the second letter (v. 8 sqq.) must be viewed as a counter-petition despatched to the same quarter, and we must think of a situation somewhat analogous to the modern practice of rival railway companies opposing each other's Bills before Parliament!

been, even if it had been continued to the extent that Ezra desired. His great weapon had fallen from his hand, and for it there was no substitute. It seems also probable that he wanted backing on the part of the local authorities. These things rendered him powerless for a time ; but only for a time.

6. Nehemiah the Governor.—Ezra's work, which bore fruit in all the subsequent history of the nation, was vigorously carried on by one who brought to bear upon it some important qualifications not possessed by himself. This was Nehemiah, the distinguished man who gives his name to the book which continues the narrative from this point. It takes the form of an autobiography, and reveals a very strenuous personality. Throughout his Court life Nehemiah had kept himself " unspotted from the world." His transparent honesty, his absolute fidelity, his unaffected piety, are mirrored in every line of his memoir. Possessed also of tact, sagacity, and wealth, he soon extended his influence over the whole community. Although of no priestly family, like Ezra, he had a strong arm and a resolute will, and was also in the good graces of the king. All this made him well fitted to advance the interests of Israel. Jerusalem had again fallen into a miserable condition. This Nehemiah learned from Hanani, his brother, who, along with some other Jews, visited him at Shushan, where he held the coveted post of king's cup-bearer. At once he patriotically resolved that, God helping him, he would go and do what he could for his nation. On a favourable opportunity presenting itself, he opened his heart to his royal master, and obtained leave to proceed to Judea as governor, with authority to restore the walls of Jerusalem. Artaxerxes also gave him an escort of " captains and horsemen," letters to the authorities of the intermediate provinces, and an order to Asaph the king's forester to supply him with timber. It was in the month Nisan, B.C. 444, that Nehemiah started on his pious mission. As he was able to announce the royal sanction, he

had little difficulty in persuading the Jews to begin the work of restoration.

7. Rebuilding of the Walls: External Opposition and Internal Difficulties.—The plan of campaign—for such it literally proved to be—was simple and thorough. The work was portioned out among separate parties to the number of about forty, all to act simultaneously, and each to be responsible for its own share. A photograph of the scene has been preserved in Neh. iii. The various sections were intrusted to men of character and position, those who were inhabitants of Jerusalem undertaking to build the portion over against their own houses. There were many helpers from all the country round, and the members of the priesthood, as well as the laity, did their part. No sooner had a beginning been made with the preliminaries to the work, than there appeared signs of opposition. This was led by three men, Sanballat the Horonite, the crafty governor of Samaria ; Tobiah the Ammonite, apparently a ransomed slave raised to authority in the house of his master ; and Geshem the Arabian, probably an independent sheikh or free-lance, for whom a fight always had its attractions. These raised the cry of rebellion against the king ; but Nehemiah resented their interference as gratuitous and insulting. Sanballat's enmity to Nehemiah was not personal, nor was it even against the Jewish race that his hatred burned. His aim was to prevent the adoption by the Jews of the policy of isolation advocated by Ezra. He wanted no " wall in Judah and in Jerusalem " which would shut out the surrounding population from the religious inheritance of Mount Zion. At first he and his confederates had been inclined to scoff. "What do these feeble Jews?" was the question with which he had entertained the Samaritan army. Tobiah, too, opined that even a jackal, should he bound on it, would break down the wall they should build. They soon ceased from their mockery, however, and resolved forcibly to interdict the work of building. A league was formed with all the neighbouring tribes jointly to attack Jerusalem, in the hope of surprising, with sudden slaughter, those at work upon the walls. But Nehemiah knew how to watch as well as pray. Whenever the enemy approached, they found the people in solid phalanx arrayed against them, and were compelled to draw off without striking a blow. Nehemiah, however, did not relax his vigilance. Every builder who plied the trowel was girt also with a sword. Day by day, "from the dawning of the morning till the stars appeared," did the work go on apace. It is not surprising that such rare devotion should have been crowned with success ; but bound up with it there was something better still. Under this experience the Jews improved immensely in nerve and tone. The discomfiture of Sanballat meant to some extent the resurrection of the national spirit of independence which had been slumbering during their long vassalage. For the first time since the Exile they tasted the sweets and felt the strength of victory.

At this stage, however, a new difficulty cropped up. To the problem of outward defence was now added that of internal reform. Happily the statesmanship that had so well organised the one was also capable of dealing with the other. The crux arose in connection with the complaints of a needy proletariat. Obliged to abandon their several occupations in order to take part in rebuilding the walls, the poorer classes were forced to mortgage their lands and enslave their families as the condition of obtaining bread and paying the royal tribute. Discouraged "because of the dearth," and exasperated by the exactions of the money-lenders, they at last gave vent to their grievances. "There was a great cry of the people, and of their wives, against their brethren the Jews." Nehemiah felt "very angry" over the pitiful revelation. His first act was deliberately to rebuke the nobles, priests, and rulers, and to denounce the practice of usury ; then, in presence of a "great assembly," he showed how differently he had himself acted, and besought them, "for fear of God, lest they should become a reproach to the heathen," to restore at once the lands and houses they had seized, and to remit a part even of their legal claims. It was a straightforward, high-toned appeal, to which the creditors felt constrained to yield. Nehemiah made them ratify their promise by an oath ; and uttered a severe malediction against those who should fail to keep it. The governor's wisdom had saved the colony. "All the people said, Amen, and praised the Lord."

The fortification of the city was now so far advanced that the national enemies determined to make a last effort to prevent its completion. They abandoned coercion for craft, and were unfortunately aided in their intrigues by the treachery of "the nobles of Judah," who were in close correspondence with Tobiah. The new governor was invited to meet Sanballat and Geshem in conference at Kephirim,[1] in the plain of Ono, near the Philistine frontier. Too shrewd a man to walk into this trap, Nehemiah pleaded in excuse the importance of his work. Four times they repeated their proposal in vain. The adversaries of Israel then resolved once more to change their tactics. The state of declension into which prophecy had now fallen enabled them to purchase prophetic aid in the matter of intimidating Nehemiah. A certain Shemaiah, at once prophet and priest, but temporarily disqualified from appearing in the temple, represented to Nehemiah that his life was in danger, and urged him to secrete himself within the sacred building, offering at the same time, despite his ceremonial defilement, to accompany and remain with him. This fresh attempt to discredit him was frustrated, however, by the courage and piety of the governor, who refused either to be a coward or a breaker of God's law.

8. Completion and Dedication of the Wall: Population of Jerusalem supplemented.—"So the wall was finished on the 25th of Elul (August, B.C. 444), in fifty-two days." With signal bravery, and with marvellous rapidity, Nehemiah had executed his great task. The moral effect of his achievement was felt in all the region round about, the enemies of Israel being much dejected

---

[1] Neh. vi. 2. It seems better (with Bertheau) to take the word as a proper name than to translate "in the villages."—A.V.

by this tangible evidence that they had been fighting against a superhuman power. Jerusalem was once more a fortified city, and it was remitted to "the porters and the singers and the Levites" to act as guards, the general administration of affairs being intrusted to Hanani, Nehemiah's brother, and Hananiah, the captain of the temple fortress. But though "the city was large and great, the people were few therein, and the houses were not builded"; and Nehemiah perceived that the next thing to be dealt with was the question of population. A census revealed the fact that, exclusive of servants, there were only 3044 adult citizens—less than a tenth of the number who had accompanied Zerubbabel from Babylon. It was therefore resolved to make up the deficiency by casting lots among the Jewish settlers in the vicinity. Every tenth man on whom the lot fell was obliged, unless some other volunteered to take his place, to transfer his household to the holy city. In adopting this plan, Nehemiah practically did for Jerusalem what Theseus had done for Athens, and Gelon for Syracuse. Some time after the completion of the walls—how long is uncertain—they were formally and joyfully dedicated to Jehovah, without whose blessing the strongest ramparts were of no avail.

9. Public Reading of the Law.—Ezra now comes once more to the front. Nothing is said as to the events which led up to his reappearance; we do not even know for certain whether the Great Scribe spent the interval in Jerusalem at all. Nehemiah's only mention of him is in connection with the dedication of the wall (xii. 36);[1] and it was about the same time that, at the popular request, he resumed his work as a teacher of the law. Long neglect had produced general ignorance as to its contents; but, wearied perhaps by the priestly ritual, the people were now thirsting for the Scriptures. An immense throng assembled on the first day of the seventh month "in the square in front of the

---

[1] Chaps. viii.-x., where there is a change from the first person to the third, being probably the work of another writer.

water-gate," and from early morning until midday listened attent-
ively while Ezra, who stood upon a lofty wooden platform, read
to them out of the "book of the law of Moses." He was supported by Nehemiah, and by thirteen priests. An equal number
of Levites were present to explain what was read. The people
showed their reverence by standing up when Ezra unrolled the
sacred parchment, as well as by their fervent Amens and devout
attitude when he led them in prayer. A band of Levites lent
their aid by reading from the new law-book "distinctly," and by
giving an Aramaic paraphrase of the passages read. The reading of the Torah produced a deep impression—"all the people
wept." They felt keenly the national degeneration that had
taken place, and the painful discrepancy between the enactments
of the law and their own practice. It was pointed out to them
by their leaders, however, that the occasion of a great festival
was essentially one for rejoicing, and that they ought to diffuse
their joy by sending seasonable gifts to the poor. This advice
was acted upon, and the mist of tears melted away in the sun-
shine of joy.

The law of God which Ezra the scribe had "in his hand" when
he first came to Jerusalem, and which he was at length enabled
to publish and put in force in or about B.C. 444, was practically
the Pentateuch as we possess it. According to the prevailing
verdict of modern criticism, the distinctively new feature of the
written law as thus promulgated was the so-called Priestly Code,[1]
which began to be drawn up by the captive priests after the
destruction of the temple. No longer able to practise the sacred
ritual, they preserved the memory of it by reducing its details to
writing. Ezekiel and others laboured at this task, and during
the Exile there arose a school of men devoted to the systematic
study and codification of the old priestly usage. There was thus
gradually produced and completed the ritual code which formed
the law of the Second Temple. This code, embodied in the

---

[1] *I.e.* the Book of Leviticus and the ceremonial sections in Exodus and
Numbers.

Pentateuch, became "the definitive Mosaic law"; and upon this as a whole, and not as previously upon the Deuteronomic legislation alone, the covenant now came to be based. This hypothesis, it should be clearly understood, does not imply that the Priestly Code was exclusively the *creation* of this period, but only that it was a readjustment of the older ritual to the altered circumstances. Thus, to use the words of a leading exponent of this view, "this double aspect of the Priests' Code is reconciled by the supposition that the chief ceremonial institutions of Israel are *in their origin* of great antiquity; but that the laws respecting them were gradually developed and elaborated, and *in the shape in which they are formulated in the Priests' Code* that they belong to the Exilic or early post-Exilic period. In its main stock, the legislation of the Priests' Code was thus not (as the critical view of it is sometimes represented by its opponents as teaching) 'manufactured' by the priests during the Exile : it is based upon *pre-existing temple usage*, and exhibits the form which that finally assumed." [1]

10. **Festival, Fast, and Covenant.** — Ezra well knew that to indoctrinate the more influential citizens with its principles, and to secure their adherence to its precepts, was half the battle as regarded the introduction of the new law-book. It is therefore not surprising to find, on the day after the festival, the chiefs of the community gathered round the Great Scribe to "consider the words of the law." One passage most appropriately submitted to them was Lev. xxiii. 39-43, containing the instructions as to the Feast of Tabernacles. Joyfully, and to the last legal detail, the people observed this feast, which had apparently been neglected since the days of Zerubbabel. It was just the season for its observance. Loads of tree-branches from the Mount of Olives were transformed into "booths"; the flat roofs, the city squares, the temple courts, were all dotted over with these picturesque erections; and for the full eight days Jerusalem was

[1] Driver, *Introduction to the Literature of the O.T.*

en fête. On every one of the days Ezra "read in the book of
the law of God," thus following up the advantage he had got.
Altogether it was a festival to be remembered, and one for which
no parallel could be found without going back to the far-off days
of Joshua and the conquest.

The feast was separated by but a single day's interval from a
solemn fast, which was observed on the 24th of the month as a
special act of national humiliation. Only Jews took part in this
function. "The seed of Israel" gathered in their thousands,
every one of them wearing the external signs of grief. They
spent three hours in listening to the words of the law, and for
another three hours they made confession of their sins. At this
stage the Levites rendered a choral ascription of praise. Then
followed from Ezra's own lips [1] an elaborate acknowledgment of
the divine goodness and justice, and a humble confession of
Israel's manifold sins. This penitential prayer took the form of
an epitome of the national history, so framed as to impress the
people with the fact that on Jehovah's side it had all along been
a history of blessing and deliverance, and on theirs one of pro-
vocation and iniquity.

That Ezra had rightly interpreted the feelings of the assembly,
was proved by the people's readiness to enter into a solemn
covenant to observe God's law. This covenant was written out
in careful terms, probably by Ezra, who was again able to make
his influence felt. It provided that there should be no intermarriage between Jews and outsiders; that there should be
no trading on Sabbaths; that every seventh year should be
signalised by a remission of debts; that the temple service
should be maintained by a yearly tax of one-third of a shekel
upon every adult male; [2] that the covenanters should take their
turn in providing fuel for the altar; and that they should duly
respect the legal obligations as to the offering of first-fruits and

---

[1] The Septuagint prefaces Neh. ix. 6 with the words: "And Ezra spake."

[2] The law (Ex. xxx. 13) prescribed half a shekel, but this seems to have
been too large an amount to levy at this time.

the payment of tithes to the priestly order. In due course there
followed the formal sealing of the covenant. Nehemiah, as
tirshatha, was the first to append his signature. Next to his
name stands that of Zedekiah, whom some suppose to have been
his secretary. Ezra's concurrence seems to have been taken for
granted ; but that of Eliashib, the high priest, was manifestly
withheld. Heads of houses, as representatives of the priests,
the Levites, and the laity, signed to the number of eighty-four,
all the rest of the people simply giving in their adherence.

11. The Last of the Prophets.—The supremacy attained by the
law inevitably led to the decline of prophecy. With the elaboration of the written code, there was no longer the same need for
the guidance of the living voice. True prophecy could have
maintained itself only as the vehicle of further revelation, and
had really no adequate function to discharge in an age when
men's minds were wholly concerned about gathering up, assimilating, and conserving the results already reached. For a time,
therefore, its work was done. The centre of authority was
changed. The influence of the prophet gave way to that of the
priest and the scribe ; the living, progressive, spoken oracle, to
the external rule of the law ; the development of doctrine, to that
of ceremonial detail. In reading Malachi we become conscious
of a transition to a new style of prophetic speech. The dialectic
skill with which this last representative of his order lays down
theses, starts questions with reference to them, and then replies
to the objections raised, already savours of the manner of the
schools. To the Socratic method he unites, moreover, somewhat
of the new legalistic spirit—that he can rise above it is evident
from chap. i. 11—denouncing marriage with Gentiles, and calling
on the people to " remember the law of Moses " (iv. 4). Through
neglect of its precepts a curse rested upon their nation (iii. 8, 9).
They had plenty of questions to ask, and of complaints to put
(ii. 17), but what was wanted was obedience to the law (iii. 7).
The priests profaned the altar by mechanically going through an

insincere service (i. 7, ii. 9); the people refused to pay the temple dues (iii. 8). Room was made for heathen wives by the divorce of the daughters of Israel, whose tears covered the altar (ii. 11-13). A sceptical spirit pervaded the community (iii. 14); sorcery, immorality, perjury, and oppression were rampant (ii. 5); the truly pious were few (iii. 16). There was widespread murmuring because Jehovah's judgment upon the heathen was delayed (ii. 17). But the Messianic deliverance, which would certainly come (iii. 1), was deferred owing to the unchanging love which would not consume the sons of Jacob (iii. 6). Meanwhile Jehovah would send His messenger, the prophet Elijah (iii. 1, iv. 5), to prepare His way, by turning the hearts of fathers and children alike, before the day when He should suddenly come to His temple and subject the covenant people to a sifting judgment that would effectually distinguish between the righteous and the wicked (iii. 18, iv. 1). Such is the last word of Old Testament prophecy. While protesting against an externalism that afterwards budded into Pharisaism, Malachi is himself tinged with the spirit of the period. His beautiful word-portrait of the true priest (ii. 6, 7) reflects the fresh conception of the scribe. And in thus signalising the entrance of the Jewish Church upon a new era, that was to last until the nation's greatest need should be supplied in the shape of a mighty prophet like Elijah, Malachi practically announced that the activity of the prophets had come to an end. Ere long this was fully recognised ; the people did not look for the perfect development of their religion until the great reformer should arise (1 Macc. xiv. 41). At first they hardly knew what a fountain of life and power had ceased to play upon the national spirit, so overjoyed were they to possess in writing the sacred praxis ; but they were yet to have ample time to discover that even this could not wholly compensate for the absence of the living messengers of Jehovah's will. Between the sunset glow of Malachi and the morning dawn, as represented in Him of whom he prophesied, there intervened the long space of 400 years. Then at length did the greatest yet born of woman, coming in the spirit and power of Elias, point to the Sun of righteousness as already risen with healing in His wings.

12. Reforms carried through by Nehemiah.—After twelve years of governorship, Nehemiah returned to King Artaxerxes, then resident, apparently, at Babylon. Here he probably resumed his former occupation, but after a short interval he was permitted to go back to Judea. The reformation effected by him did not stand the test of his absence. Deeply mortified to discover this, he began *de novo.* To cleanse a desecrated temple was the first business laid to his hand. Eliashib had proved a singularly traitorous high priest. He not only did not disdain to "ally himself unto Tobiah," but had even placed at the disposal of this foreigner one of the temple chambers. As heathen occupant of Jehovah's house, Tobiah was to the zealous governor still more repulsive than he had formerly been as conspirator against his own life. His furniture was cleared out of the chamber so sacrilegiously allotted to him, and, after it had been purified, the tithes and other priestly provisions were stored in it as aforetime. The desecration of the temple had not unnaturally been accompanied by the desecration of the Sabbath, and Nehemiah, determined that this abuse also should be rectified, gave orders that the city gates should be closed from Friday at dusk until Saturday at sunset. There remained still another evil to which the newly returned *tirshatha* was not blind. Intermarriage with Gentiles had again become general. Nehemiah "saw Jews that had married wives of Ashdod, of Ammon, and of Moab." Their children spoke a mongrel dialect in which Hebrew was jumbled up with "the speech of Ashdod." The governor's treatment of the defaulters was very severe, and he made them swear that such marriages should no longer be contracted. One painful feature about this defection was that the leading reactionaries were found among priestly families. A grandson of Eliashib's was son-in-law to Sanballat, and flatly refused to dissolve his marriage with Nicaso, his alien wife. The indignant Nehemiah "chased him" from his presence, and expelled him from Jerusalem, as one who had "defiled the priest-hood."

13. The Samaritan Schism.—The Manasseh whom Josephus (*Ant.* xi. 8) mentions as founder of the Samaritan temple was doubtless this same excommunicated priest, although he erroneously ascribes the incident to the time of Alexander the Great. A considerable number of Judeans, both lay and clerical, made common cause with Manasseh. The laxer portion of the community refused to sacrifice their natural affections to the dictates of a severely exclusive and unbending rule, conceived though it was in the interests of a pious patriotism. They pre-ferred to sever their connection with the new colony, and betook themselves to the Samaritans. To the powerful Sanballat this Jewish secession opened up a new vista towards the fulfilment of his hopes. The new-comers could furnish a copy of the Pentateuch and a high priest of Aaron's line. What need then of further parley? Sanballat determined that Samaria should have a temple of its own, around which the spirit of nationality might grow. From this date, accordingly, no more friendly overtures were made to the Jews by the Samaritans, who now became a separate religious sect. They built an independent temple on Mount Gerizim, and boldly attempted to transfer thither the glorious traditions of Zion—an attempt in which they have persisted even to the present day.[1] Ever since their foundation they have claimed a monopoly of the true religion of Moses, accepting as Holy Scripture nothing beyond the Pentateuch, which they possess in a text for the most part identical with that of the Jews. The rite of circumcision, the Sabbath, and the yearly Jewish festivals, are duly observed by them. But they renounce the Jewish

[1] Stapfer (*Palestine in the Time of Christ*, p. 124) asserts that the Samaritans are now extinct ; but this is not the case. According to the Quarterly State-ment of the Palestine Exploration Fund for January 1888, the number of Samaritans now living is 165. This accords also with the estimates given by travellers in still more recent years.

sanctuary and priesthood as unauthorised and schismatic, maintaining that not Zion but Gerizim is the place of God's choice. There Joshua had been commanded of old to build a temple ; and that "this mountain" is still the place where men ought to worship, they prove by reading Gerizim for Ebal in their Pentateuch (Deut. xxvii. 4). The breach thus made was never healed. In the new cultus on Gerizim the Samaritans gave to their hatred "a local habitation and a name." Not only did they shun all social intercourse with Jews, and, as in the case of our Lord Himself, refuse to harbour them (Luke ix. 52) ; they even attacked bands of pilgrims on their way to Jerusalem, defiled the temple with dead bodies, and kindled false beacon-fires on their mountain tops to deceive the Babylonian settlers, who looked for such signals from their countrymen in Judah on the first appearance of the Paschal moon. The Jews were equally bitter on their side, reproaching the Samaritans with their heathen origin, and assailing their worship as idolatrous, their character as mendacious. To taste a morsel of Samaritan food was an abomination like the eating of swine's flesh.[1] The recorded sayings of the Rabbis prove the severity of the ostracism practised on this alien race.[2] "If anyone receive a Cuthean into his house, and show him hospitality, he is simply preparing exile for his sons." "Mius ben Ihi said, May I never hold intercourse with a Cuthean ; but Abo ben Ihi said, May I never set eyes on a Cuthean." The state of Jewish feeling is also well illustrated in the taunt thrown out to Jesus, "Thou art a Samaritan, and hast a devil"—these being viewed as convertible terms.

A direct challenge was thus given to the Judeans to prove themselves the people of God ; and they knew that henceforth they had nothing to expect but hatred and annoyance from the quarter

---

[1] Lightfoot, *Horæ Hebraicæ*, p. 993. There were, however, some differences in the degree of exclusiveness on this point, as may be inferred from the fact that Jesus let His disciples buy meat in Samaria (John iv. 8). Lightfoot quotes *Hieros. Avoda Zara*, fol. 44. 4 : "Victualia Cuthæorum permissa sunt, si non immisceatur iis aliquid vini eorum, aut aceti."

[2] Compare the epithet ἀλλογενής applied to them by Christ (Luke xvii. 18).

whence the challenge came. The rival communities tried to outdo each other in gaining the favour of the successive conquerors of Palestine. Both set up a claim of right to the name and privilege of the ancient Israelitish nation. They were too nearly equal in strength to allow of the suppression of the one by the other, and so they lived on to harass and persecute each other to the utmost.

14. Consolidation of Judaism under Ezra and Nehemiah.—With the establishment of the spurious worship in Gerizim there disappeared, however, one danger which had been threatening the Jews—that of syncretism. Amid the general wreckage of contemporary religious and national usages, Judaism remained a distinct entity. Bereft of the usual attributes of nationality, the Jews yet held together in virtue of their law. They gradually gained so many adherents in Palestine, that the Aramaic dialect now began to supersede the older Hebrew. The speech of trade and diplomacy, it ousted Hebrew as Arabic has in turn ousted it.

Nehemiah's memoirs close with the characteristic prayer : " Remember me, O my God, for good." The curtain drops here upon the life of this zealous man. He was the civil, as Ezra was the ecclesiastic, patriot of his age. In the case of both, the circumstances of their death are unknown to us. Several legendary stories are connected with the name of the powerful governor. The statement of Josephus, that Ezra " died an old man, and was buried in a magnificent manner at Jerusalem," probably rests only on the popular belief. There is a Talmudic tradition that he died in Persia. For a time the reputation of the Great Scribe seems to have been overshadowed by that of Nehemiah : in Ecclesiasticus (xlix.) only the latter is named in the list of "famous men." But as time rolled on the two reformers came to be seen in their true perspective, and as the influence of the scribes increased, Ezra especially was considered great. Revered as a second Moses,[1] he was invested with the authority of a prophet, and accorded the position of an independent lawgiver. Portions of the Pentateuch,

---

[1] Cf. 2 Apoc. Ezra xiv. 10, where a voice addresses Esdras *out of a bush*.

as well as other parts of Scripture, were ascribed to his pen. It is beyond dispute that under Ezra the written law became a new power in Israel; and the inference that to his labours we are under God, indebted for the preservation of not a little of the sacred text, is a warrantable one. The order of the scribes owes its origin to him, and we are probably to trace to the same source the important institution of the synagogue. Ezra's influence thus lived on after his death, and became far greater than it had been during his lifetime. Conjointly with Nehemiah, he had effected a restoration which practically amounted to the consolidation of Judaism. In re-establishing the law to the extent of its possible observance, the Great Scribe had shown the Jewish people wherein lay their strength, had endowed them with an imperishable possession, had filled them with a quiet determination never again to forsake the path of their true development, and had put them at last in a position patiently to wait for the advent of Christ.

15. Close of the Persian Dominion.—Artaxerxes died in B.C. 424, after a peaceful reign of forty years. His successors did not share his consideration for the Jewish people or the Jewish faith. Most of them were worthless characters, and some of them positively brutal and wicked. Almost every corner of the empire became the scene of discontent and insurrection. The expedition of the "Ten Thousand"[1] had disclosed the military weakness of Persia. Cyprus, Egypt, and Phœnicia made a combined although abortive effort to throw off the imperial dominion. But the war was carried on by the chiefs of Asia Minor and others. This must have borne hard upon Judea, as a part of the province which more than any other was devastated by the sanguinary conflicts of the period. Although we know next to nothing of the Jewish settlers under the successors of Artaxerxes, there is reason to suppose that it was now theirs to groan under the yoke of Persia as their fathers had done under that of Babylon. Among the scattered facts which give indication of

[1] For detailed account, see Xenophon's *Anabasis*.

this, may be mentioned the destruction of Jericho by Ochus, the attempt of the foreign superiors to take into their own hands the appointment of the high priest, the taxation of the daily sacrifices, and the transportation by Artaxerxes III. of a number of Jews to the Caspian seaboard. But the civil commotions of the time made little impact upon the now solid structure of the Jewish Church. Every year saw the breach widen religiously as well as politically between the colony at Jerusalem and the nation whose vassals they were. The religion of the earlier Persians was not without its high qualities, or even without some affinity to Judaism ; but in these later and more degenerate days, especially under Mnemon and Ochus, it was mixed up with elements that made every true-hearted Jew recoil from its adherents. The downfall of the Persian dominion was, however, at hand. The wonder is that the huge colossus staggered so long ere it fell, for moral and material decay are never far separated. The victorious son of Philip the Macedonian king was on the march : and first on the banks of the Granicus, then on the plain of Issus, and finally at the battle of Arbela, he defeated the demoralised and disorganised Persians, and so decided the fate of the great Monarchy that had held sway in the East for more than two hundred years.

CHAPTER IV

INNER LIFE OF ISRAEL DURING THE PERSIAN PERIOD

The life of the nation was developed by the interaction of forces from without and forces from within. The external forces were the foreign influences to which it was subjected ; and the internal forces consisted of those imperishable impulses which sprang from their own Messianic hope, and embodied themselves in the institutions of the period.

1. **The Introduction of Foreign Elements.**—The Chaldeans had exercised no appreciable influence upon the religion of the Old Testament. If the pious Jew borrowed anything at all from Babylon, it was the visionary mode of speech with which Ezekiel has familiarised us. There was, of course, much more affinity between the religion of the Jews and that of the Persians ; but it may be questioned whether the Persian influence on Old Testament doctrine was of a very strongly-marked character. We can pass from Ezekiel to Haggai or Zechariah without being conscious of the introduction of any foreign elements of importance. Persians and Jews were undoubtedly at one in their monotheism and in their hatred of idolatry. But to say that the Jews derived such fundamental doctrines as those of immortality and the resurrection from the system of Zoroaster, is to overstate the Persian influence. If in the passage mainly relied on to support this view—Dan. xii.—there be any distinct advance upon such older statements as those of Ps. xvi. and Job xix., must we necessarily ascribe it to the adoption of Zoroastrian tenets? The doctrine of the resurrection is an organic product of Old Testament religion. Only in non-essentials, and especially in the matter of angelology, is the Persian influence traceable. The main features of Zoroastrianism were its doctrine of the co-existence of good and evil as eternal and antagonistic principles, and its extraordinary use of numbers and images. Out of these tempting materials Judaism now sought to weave for itself an ornamental fringe, so to speak, but that was all. An instance of this occurs in Zechariah's picture of the new Jerusalem (iii. 9, iv. 10). To the poetic imagination the spirit-world began to be peopled with hierarchies of good and evil powers, a tendency that developed until it affected even ordinary prose narrative (1 Chron. xxi. 1). It is not observable in Ezekiel, who, with all his fondness for images, makes no mention of evil spirits. Another fact to be noted in this connection, is that even among Jews it now became a regular practice to date events by the year of the reigning Persian king.

2. Nature and Growth of the High-Priestly Power.—A notable factor in the development of Judaism during the Persian period was that of the priesthood. But while the age was an age of priests, the one figure that stands out with incomparable prominence is the head of the hierarchy. It was now that the high-priestly power began to assume the unique supremacy which it afterwards attained. Under the kings of Judah and Israel, the high priest held an honourable yet subordinate position. Even in his own department he had been subject to the king; but now he held his office directly from Jehovah, whose earthly representative he was. Other things, too, combined to make the office a new centre of influence. Its ancient prestige as a relic of the former constitution; the principle of heredity, according to which Joshua's successors were his own descendants; and the life-tenure attaching to the appointment, all told in this direction. Although the Urim and Thummim had vanished, and the holy oracle could no longer be consulted as of yore, the people yet saw in the high priest their natural head. And thus, without his ever claiming it, secular power also drifted into his hands. No other dignitary could find a place by his side. He was leader of the community, not only religiously, but socially and politically as well. From the account given in Sirach of the son of Onias, we can gather how influential was the position of this functionary when his worth as a man at all corresponded to the dignity of the office. Unhappily this was not always the case. The conditions already mentioned opened up opportunities for self-seeking, and many of the high priests made their office a ladder to personal power. The post of civil governor in Jerusalem, which had been held by Nehemiah, seems to have been subsequently abolished, the Persian satrap of Syria deeming it expedient to vest the entire secular authority in the person of the high priest. An incident recorded by Josephus shows us the new arrangement apparently in actual operation. Judas, the son of Eliashib, died, leaving two sons, Johanan and Joshua, both of whom sought to obtain

the office demitted by their father. Johanan, as the elder, held
the legal title, but Joshua was the nominee of Bagoses, the acting
Persian general, who was his friend. Relying on this influential
support, Joshua provoked his brother to a quarrel, and was slain
by him within the sacred precincts. Bagoses immediately went
to Jerusalem and forced his way into the sanctuary. The Jews
raised the cry of profanation, but he retorted that he was cleaner
than a murdered body, and as a punishment for this fratricide
he imposed on them for seven years a tax of fifty shekels
(drachmas)[1] for every lamb used in sacrifice. From all this it
is obvious that the increased political importance of the priesthood was not an unmixed blessing to the Jewish people. It
led to moral degeneracy, as it did in the parallel case of the
Papacy during the Middle Ages. Under such a system the
high priest frequently cared less for his sacred office than for
the worldly influence which it carried with it. Not that
this was true of all the high priests ; some of them were what
they were expected to be—the visible embodiment of "the
divine purity and joy." But after the Persian dominion had
passed away, the evil results of the system became more
apparent.

3. **The Scribes and their Traditions.** — The most potent
influence in the national development must be sought, however,
in connection with the new order of professional students of the
law, named *Sopherim* or Scribes. These men were lawyers,
teachers, and judges, all in one. Jerusalem being conceived as
the Holy City, a growing importance was assigned to the Holy
Scriptures, especially to the law. It became from the time of
Ezra the centre of thought and religion in Judea—the recognised
embodiment of all wisdom, and the venerated palladium of the
people. The highest employment open to an Israelite was
the study and interpretation of it. Diligent hands wrote out
numerous copies, and so arose the office of the Sopherim. What

[1] The total amount for the seven years would be about £12,000.

was best, as well as what was worst in Judaism, was henceforth represented by this order.

The scribes were a learned caste, located all over Palestine, but having their headquarters at Jerusalem. As guardians of the law, they formed a guild with common interests, and maintained their authority by observing uniformity in their teaching. Originally they sprang from the priesthood. It belonged to the priestly function to expound the law (Mal. ii. 7), and to settle questions regarding it (Hag. ii. 11); but the law had now such a position in Israel that the study of it necessarily became an independent avocation. The moral influence of the hierarchs passed thus into the hands of the Rabbis, who were for the most part earnest-minded laymen. They were held in the greatest public esteem, and demanded of their pupils a reverence exceeding even that accorded to parents.[1] Usually they gave their services free of charge, and supported themselves by practising a trade. They were furnished with rooms in the temple porches, where they sat and taught.

The basis of Scribism was the claim that every Jew was bound to obey the law in all its particulars. It was the acceptance of this responsibility, and the attempt to discharge it, that marked off the Jew from other men. One might Judaise himself and establish his own righteousness by laborious conformity to legal enactment. This became indeed the one occupation of the pious, for to do everything by rule was of the essence of Judaism. An encyclopædia of human conduct can never be written, although the scribes contrived to do it to the utmost extent possible. Despite omissions, seeming contradictions, and changing circumstances, they set themselves by processes of inference to bring every conceivable case within the range of the law, that the piously-disposed Jew might be at no loss how to perform the obligations of the covenant. The effect of Scribism was thus to multiply the legal points to be attended to in the conduct of life, until the burden got to be intolerable. The

[1] Cf. Matt. xxiii. 6, 7.

written law contained 613 commandments; but obedience to these by no means exhausted the religious obligations of a Jew. The Rabbis assert—and to this day Jewish children are taught —that God gave to Moses on Sinai not only the written law, but also an equally binding oral law. This latter is usually designated the traditional law, or *Halachah*.[1] According to the *Pirke Aboth*, Moses "delivered it to Joshua; he to the elders; the elders to the prophets; and the prophets to the men of the Great Assembly," of whom Haggai (B.C. 520) was the first, and Simon the Just (B.C. 300) the last. From Simon's time the precious tradition passed by an unbroken succession of pairs of learned men (whose names are preserved) to the Christian era. The ever-increasing body of oral tradition thus handed down from master to scholar was finally embodied in the Talmud. It cannot be said that the devotion of the Jews to their sacred tradition did much either for the higher learning or the higher life; but such as it is, the Talmud represents the cumulative labours of 500 years. Although often referred to as a useless pile of rubbish, it illustrates in many ways the inner life of the Jewish people during the centuries preceding the birth of Christ, and helps us to understand His position as a public Teacher opposed to the Rabbis and their traditions.

If mere law could ever sustain the religious life of a people, the endless casuistry of the scribes would have accomplished this for Israel. But they failed, because religion is neither an art to be learned nor a trade to be wrought at, but a principle to be imbibed. Here it was that Jesus of Nazareth joined issue with the scribes. To what they considered of most importance, He gave only a secondary place, and taught that the spirit must be left to express itself in forms of its own creation. He charged them with having developed the law in a wrong direction altogether, and with having by their traditions made it void. The inward life and freedom of the divine word lay buried

[1] Literally, *that which goes*, and hence applied to *the law of custom*.

beneath a load of outward precepts. This marks the fundamental difference between Christianity and the traditionalism
of the schools. Scribism meant externalism, and fostered
the worship of the letter at the expense of the better worship of the spirit. It produced a purely artificial piety,
which was concerned only with the doing of what was prescribed.[1] In such an atmosphere both morality and religion
were stifled.

4. The Synagogue.—It was in keeping with the new spirit
accompanying the restoration of the law, that this period should
also have seen the land dotted over with synagogues. Tradition
ascribed to them a much earlier origin, but they were really an
outgrowth of the post-Exilian age. By the time of Christ the
synagogue was an old-established institution. Every village in
Palestine had long had its meeting-house (Acts xv. 21) ; and this
was the case throughout the Dispersion also. The expense of
building and maintaining these "houses of God" seems to have
been borne by the worshippers in each district ; although sometimes poor congregations were indebted to the munificence of
private individuals for a place of worship (Luke vii. 5). Synagogues were often built on the seashore, or beside some stream,
to facilitate Levitical purification. In the choice of sites, preference was also shown for hills (Luke iv. 28, 29), street corners,
"the openings of the gates," and in later times for "the
sepulchres of the righteous" (Matt. xxiii. 29). Regard was had
in all cases to the *Kibleh*, or fixed direction of worship, Jerusalem
being in this respect to the Jew what Mecca is to the Moham-
medan. The spot on which a synagogue was built could never be
used for any secular purpose. In the large towns there were

---

[1] "A late scribe gave apt expression to the genius of the whole school,
when he declared that the great commandment of the law was the law about
fringes. Take care of the fringes, and the garment will take care of itself :
keep the little commandments, and you cannot break the great ones ;—that
was the spirit in which the scribes developed the law of God."—Skinner,
Historical Connection between the Old and New Testaments, p. 16.

several of these structures,[1] which varied, like our modern churches, in size and style of architecture.

The internal arrangements were very simple, although modelled somewhat after those of the temple. Corresponding to the outer court was the space allotted to the body of the people, who took their places according to rank and age. The sexes sat apart. In the raised platform which took up the remaining room we have the analogue of the inner court. At the further extremity, pointing towards Jerusalem, was the ark containing the holy books, and in front of it hung a curtain in imitation of the veil of the temple. The chief seats were appropriated by the leading officials, the leisured elders, the scribes (Matt. xxiii. 6), and the vulgar rich (Jas. ii. 2, 3), who liked to have a reputation for piety (Matt. vi. 2), and to sit facing the congregation. Further forward, and in a central position, was the raised seat for the reader or preacher, and the desk on which rested the sacred parchments. Among the other fittings were lamps, alms-boxes, a chest for musical instruments, and boards for writing up the names of the excommunicated.

A Sabbath morning service began with the recitation of the Shema,[2] which consisted of three paragraphs from the Pentateuch. It was a confession of faith rather than a prayer, and was preceded and concluded with a benediction. Then with the formula, "Let us bless Jehovah," the reader summoned the people to pray. This they did standing, their faces turned towards Jerusalem. The prayer, which formed part of an established liturgy, was said by the leader, the congregation giving the responsive Amen. Next came the lessons from the law,[3] and the

---

[1] "Large families often had synagogues of their own. Thus in the East to-day we find a number of mosques quite out of proportion to the population, many of them being family mosques. Sometimes a corporation founded a synagogue. We know that the coppersmiths in Jerusalem had established one."—Stapfer, *Palestine in the Time of Christ*, p. 335.

[2] So called from the opening word of Deut. vi. 4-9, xi. 13-21; Num. xv. 37-41.

[3] The Torah was divided into 154 sections, so as to admit of the entire Pentateuch being overtaken in a cycle of three years.

prophets (Luke iv. 17), with Aramaic translation.[1] This was followed by an expository sermon from a scribe or other competent male worshipper. Finally, the blessing was pronounced by a priest, or, in the absence of a priest, invoked by a layman, whereupon the congregation dispersed. The leading feature in this service was that of instruction in the law. "To hear the law and to learn it accurately"—that was the chief end for which the people congregated. But every synagogue was also a house of prayer, in which the worshippers realised that nearness to God does not depend upon a gorgeous ritual.

A great national institution like the synagogue had to be well organised. The general management was in the hands of a body of elders, who watched over the morals of the flock and exercised discipline. Every synagogue had its "ruler"; sometimes there were several in the same synagogue (Acts xiii. 15). They were managing directors, to whom was committed the general oversight of worship. Other officers of subordinate rank were the business secretary, who usually recited the prayers ; the collectors of alms, whose duty it was to receive and distribute the weekly offering ; and the attendant or minister, whose functions were to take charge of the sacred books, to open and close the synagogue and see to its being properly kept, to teach the children to read, and to scourge those who had been sentenced to receive stripes (Acts xxii. 19 ; 2 Cor. xi. 24). In addition to these were the "ten unemployed men," who were paid to give constant attendance during the hours of public worship, so as to ensure that there would always be a congregation.

As affecting the religious life of the people, the synagogue was an institution of the highest moment. It was the nursery of Mosaism ; by means of it the rank and file of the nation attained to the knowledge of the law. It made them practically independent of the temple and its ritual, freed them from the domination of the priestly hierarchy, and gave them a portable religion.

[1] This was known as the Targum, while the translator was called the Methurgeman.

Josephus pointed out with truth, that while the Roman procurators could not go to their provinces unaccompanied by legal experts, "in the Jewish household every servant-maid knew from the religious service what Moses had ordained in the law in every single instance." Notable also is the warm tribute of Philo : " Our houses of prayer in the several towns are none other than institutions for teaching prudence and bravery, temperance and justice, piety and holiness ; in short, every virtue which the human and the divine recognises and enjoins."

Christianity itself owes not a little to the synagogue. The lessons read from the prophets prepared the way of the Lord by creating and intensifying in many hearts the Messianic hope ; and when the Messiah Himself did come, He preached freely in the synagogues. The apostles made use of the same medium for the propagation of Christian doctrine. Our modern sermon is just a development of the Midrash, or homily of the synagogue. The early Church was simply the synagogue Christianised ; the resemblance extended both to the style of building and to the form of worship. In this Jewish institution we see the master-stroke of Ezra's genius, and the bridge by which Christianity crossed over on its mission of blessing to all families of the earth.

5. Germs of Future Sectarianism.—In Judea the balance of power was gradually shifting. Hitherto it had rested with the priests ; henceforth it was to drift increasingly into the hands of the scribes. These were the two most influential classes, and they both sought to get the nation under their control. During the Persian period, and for at least half a century longer, the priests maintained their supremacy ; they might have done so to the end but for their unfaithfulness to their sacred trust. It was the spiritual poverty of the priesthood, their lack of national feeling, and their unscrupulous conduct, that gave nerve and sinew to the opposition, which crystallised at length into a distinct party. Their official status could not compensate for their

lack of piety. The earnest-minded chose to hold by the men who held by the law, and as the apostles of Judaism the scribes found their influence daily increase. When the priests were afterwards fascinated by the subtle attractions of Greek culture and art, and were freely embracing practices foreign to the spirit of their own religion, the scribes were so successful in hoisting the flag of danger as to prove the saviours of their country. They fought Hellenism until the madness of Antiochus Epiphanes came to their aid, and caused the extraordinary revival of Judaism under the Maccabees. In New Testament times the scribes are found naturally among the Pharisees, and the priests as naturally adhering to the Sadducees. These opposing parties were the developed product of tendencies already at work in the Persian age, and these tendencies were themselves consequent upon the decay of spiritual power which characterised the period. The loss of this meant the loss of many things, and, among others, of that religious unity which had for generations enabled the little Jewish nation to present a solid front towards the pagan world outside. Where men are no longer agreed in their philosophy of religion or of life, the development of party feeling is inevitable.

6. **Results attained during the Persian Period.**—Two centuries had passed since the Jews returned from exile. Their bright expectations had not been realised. The hostility shown by Assyria and Babylon towards the Jewish sanctuary had certainly not been continued under the Persian Empire; and despite the petty limitations and annoyances to which they had been subjected, the new community remained gratefully conscious of the service done to the cause of the theocracy by the permission to rebuild the waste places of Zion. In other respects, however, they hardly fared better than they had done before. The goal was not yet ! Depression sat on the brow of the nation. Many began to pessimise : all was "vanity and vexation of spirit." The literature of the period felt the incubus as much as any other department

of the national life. Neither in quantity nor in quality was it equal to that of the earlier times. In the history itself, moreover, there are many blanks. Yet it would be a mistake to set down these two hundred years as a day of small things to be despised. They were years of the highest significance for Judaism, and the seeds then planted were not uprooted by the conflicts of succeeding centuries. Among the results attained were these : (1) The age was characterised by an *intense devotion to the law*. This was the engrossing study of the best heads, the centre of endeavour for the noblest wills, in Israel. The promulgation of the Torah turned the Jewish nation into a hive of workers. They laboured to master its precepts, and to reduce them to practice. And this reverence for the law was surely something gained, notwithstanding that they mistook the means for the end. Redemption could not come along the lines of legalism. There is something tragic about the Herculean zeal with which the scribes consecrated their strength to the maintenance of a lost cause. Like that of Hypatia and of Julian in a later age, it was a "zeal not according to knowledge." (2) *A higher conception of worship* was another of the distinct gains of this period. The synagogue, in practically obliterating the distinction between priest and layman, did much to create a more spiritual idea of worship than that represented in the symbolism of the temple ritual. Fellowship with God, they found, could be had directly through His word and prayer. Without priest or Levite, without animal offering or hidden type, the pious Israelite could now draw near to God. (3) During this period there was also a notable *growth of national feeling*. The idea of Israel as the chosen people became exceedingly prominent after the Exile. She was God's turtle dove (Ps. lxxiv. 19). "Touch not Mine anointed, and do My prophets no harm"—such was the glorious motto with which a divine hand had wreathed her crown. On the other hand, stung by the treatment they had received from them, the Jews now began also energetically to hate and despise the heathen as fools and enemies of God (Ps. lxxiv. 18). Babylon and Edom were the objects of a hatred peculiarly fierce (Ps. cxxxvii.). In the rejection of the advances made by the Samaritans, in the expulsion of the foreign wives under Ezra and Nehemiah, and in the story told in the Book of Esther, we have other concrete examples of this tendency. In spite of the unlovely features mixed up with it, all this meant a certain accession of moral and religious strength. Though shorn of their power as an independent nationality, they were the conscious possessors of the only true religion, and this in the end would bring the truest supremacy. All nations would yet flock to the mountain of the Lord's house. The Plant of renown must first spring up, however, before this hope could be fulfilled. They had still to look to the future for this. If meanwhile they were an oppressed people, they realised that their vocation was a far higher one than simply to be a unit among many nations. (4) The Persian period was further distinguished by the cordial *recognition of the sovereignty of holiness.* The Israelites could now dispense with the outward monarchy they were once so anxious for. They could even accept the heathen dominion as a passing experience. A lofty consciousness of their position as Jehovah's people, holy through separation, lifted them above such relations as these. It was by laying hold on the eternal, the true, and the holy, and by that alone, that they could arrive at national perfection. This was the great power that was now to have sway over them. Their ancestral faith was all they had saved from the wreck of the Exile, and perhaps it was all that was worth saving. At all events, it was the one thing needful for them in the carrying out of the divine purpose of salvation for themselves and for the world. This holiness, then, was to be the starting-point of a new development for Israel. Whatever the hollowness of the religious life in many quarters may have been, the system itself could not yield perfect results, " for the law maketh nothing perfect." It had, however, " a shadow of good things to come," and the people of the Old Covenant were gradually moving on towards those good things.

7. Jewish Literature of the Persian Period.—Towards the close of the Exile there had been something of a renaissance both in prophecy and in general literature, but the oppression of the Persian rule checked its further development. Prophecy had ceased, and although there was no want of books (Eccles. xii. 12), they were mostly of a comparatively inferior order. In the historical field a new feature appears in the autobiographies of Ezra and Nehemiah. These are embraced in the larger work of the Chronicler, who also inserts in his history the texts of royal edicts affecting the national life. This writer sketches in a Levitical spirit the course of the divine kingdom from the creation down to the rebuilding of Jerusalem after the Exile. Of the prophetic books which fall within this period, those of Haggai and Zechariah are earlier by nearly a century than that of Malachi. There are substantial grounds for ascribing to this age the puzzling Book of Ecclesiastes. In general tone and standpoint it seems to fit in with the circumstances of the Persian rather than with those of the later Græco-Syrian rule. The apocryphal books of Baruch and Tobit are perhaps also to be assigned to the Persian age. But the best literature of the period belongs to the sphere of sacred song. Although it is not easy to distinguish the psalms of this from those of the succeeding age, it would seem, from the way in which quotations are made from the Books of Chronicles,[1] that the bulk of the later psalms had their origin in the Persian period. These hymns of faith and hope are charged throughout with the feeling of the peerless value of the true religion. For the human soul it means safety (xci. 10), rest (cxvi. 7), and blessedness (cxxxix. 17); it is for the individual the chief good, and affords for the nation that possesses it the best security (cviii. 13) and .the truest happiness (cxliv. 15). There were, however, unmistakable signs that Jewish literature was on the wane. The nation had begun to live on the past.[2] A race of scholastics

---

[1] Ps. cv. and cvi. are cited in 1 Chron. xvi. 8–36, and Ps. cxxxii. in 2 Chron. vi. 41, 42.

[2] "Even poets were fond of topics from ancient history, and employed

collected and edited the classical works of former times. Artificial arrangement took the place of creative energy ; the writer who could hardly produce a poem could put together an acrostic. Every literary device was in request. Zoroastrian images and numbers came into vogue ; writings were issued under the name of some great man of a former age ; even the reversal of the order of the alphabet was a welcome novelty.[1]

them at some length in songs for every kind of instruction and exhortation."
—Ewald, *History of Israel*, v. p. 191.   Ps. xcix. and cxxxii. are cases in point.   Detailed references to the past occur also in Neh. ix. 7-47, xiii. 18, 26.

[1] This was known as the *Atbash*, so called from the first two pairs of letters interchanged, viz. *a* and *t*, *b* and *sh*.

BOOK III

THE GREEK PERIOD, B.C. 333-167

———+———

CHAPTER I

ALEXANDER'S EMPIRE

1. **Alexander the Great.**—While yet a youth of twenty, Alexander was crowned King of Macedonia. Born at Pella (B.C. 356), he became at thirteen the pupil of Aristotle, and remained ever after the faithful devotee of Greek culture. After asserting his position against rivals in Macedonia, he entered upon his work of conquest. His first achievement was the subjugation of Greece. He then marched into Asia with 40,000 well-disciplined soldiers. Meeting the Persian troops near the river Granicus, he utterly annihilated them (B.C. 334).[1] His next step was to make sure of Asia Minor, on the coasts of which two able generals commanded the fleet of Darius (Codomannus). At Halicarnassus alone did he encounter serious resistance. Leaving one of his generals to besiege its citadel, he made himself master of the Southern provinces, and was now ready to follow out his design of humbling the Great King himself. That monarch, who still underrated his enemy, paid no attention to tactics ; he left Alexander's handful of Greeks a free course until he could

[1] For an account of Alexander's tactics, pursued at this and succeeding battles, see Professor Mahaffy's work on *Alexander's Empire*, pp. 15, 16.

effectually crush them on the Syrian plain. The Macedonian did not, however, arrive so soon as he had expected, and the impatient monarch, having abandoned his advantageous position, was defeated at Issus in Cilicia (B.C. 333). Alexander now made for Phœnicia, which fell into his hands after a seven months' siege of Tyre. The victor then turned to Egypt, taking Palestine on the way, and spending two months in besieging Gaza, which paid dearly for its resistance. Egypt was quite ready to change its ruler, and the city of Alexandria remains to this day the peaceful monument of his visit to that country. Alexander had already announced himself as King of Persia, and only one other decisive blow was required to give him the undisputed lordship of Asia. This was struck (B.C. 331) at Arbela in Mesopotamia. The conqueror now entered in succession the four great capitals of the Persian Empire, and drained them of their treasures. His marriage with Roxana, the daughter of a Sogdian prince, solved his difficulties in the Northern provinces. Alexander's watch-word was still Eastward-ho! Over the heights of the Hindu Kush, through the passes of Kabul and Khyber, across the rivers Indus and Hydaspes, in the face of every obstacle he led his troops, conquering the bravest of Indian armies, and confidently expecting in a few days more to reach the Ganges itself. But at this point his hardy Macedonians failed him; they declined to go further, and the king was obliged to turn his back upon the East. In Alexander the lust of conquest grew by what it fed on; he was essentially a man-hunter. Arabia seems to have been the next item on his programme, and with a view to this campaign he ordered new ships to be built in Phœnicia and Babylon (B.C. 331). To the latter he made his way in spite of priestly presages of danger, and amid the homage of ambassadors from all parts of the world. But the limits of his empire, which now extended from the Nile to the Indus, had been reached; he had, as it were, but made a beginning when there came the sufficiently inglorious end. A prolonged drunken revel induced an attack of fever. The army viewed the situation with the utmost alarm.

Oracles were consulted; bulletins were issued; and when the Great King was no longer able to speak, his Macedonians marched past his bedside and sorrowfully bade him farewell. A few hours afterwards he was dead, and the greatest career the world had yet seen was ended.

2. Alexander's Character, Policy, and Place in History. — In point of military genius Alexander certainly merits the epithet of *Great*, but in the sphere of character he has no claim to it. With loftier ends in view perhaps than most conquerors, he nevertheless allowed the teachings of Aristotle to be overborne by ambition. Probably he became intoxicated by his unheard of success; it is impossible otherwise to account for his fatuous notion that he was divine.[1] In reality he was very far from being even what Spinoza was called, a "God-intoxicated" man. The untamable fierceness of the tiger, the brutal disregard of the Oriental for human life, the coarse excess of the Thracian reveller, the heartless tyranny of the ancient despot, were all exemplified in him. No doubt it ought to be remembered that his history has not been written by a contemporary, and that the fabulous element has entered into it largely.

Alexander's policy is summed up in two words—conquest and fusion. To build up one mighty kingdom, in which victors and vanquished alike should be embraced, and which should be permeated by the spirit and civilisation of Greece, was the ruling idea of this remarkable man. This, however, was a work demanding more than great ability and tenacity of purpose: it could scarcely even be inaugurated apart from an exceptionally long reign. His death at thirty-three necessarily left it incomplete (B.C. 323).

But life is not really measured by days and years, and

---

[1] Plutarch says that Alexander's claim to divinity was not believed in by himself; that it was with great caution and in a small degree asserted among the Greeks; and that he only used it as a weapon for the subjugation of barbarians.

Alexander has left his mark in history. He occupies indeed a unique position in the annals of the human race. To him directly are to be traced the two great movements which prepared the way for Christianity, viz. the Jewish Dispersion, and the spread of Hellenic culture among Orientals. The significance of this monarch's life for biblical history is not therefore exhausted by the place he fills in the visions of Daniel or in the pages of 1 Maccabees. He had a vocation as a revolutionary. Through his conquests a way was opened up for the fusion of the diverse tendencies and thoughts of East and West, and this again was to result in nothing less than the development of a cosmopolitan religion for man. But if the upheaval of ancient racial ideas and customs which followed in the wake of his army, and the clear-cut antagonisms of Greek and Semitic thought which were thereby revealed, constitute Alexander a sort of forerunner of Christianity, yet, by his acceptance of the idolatrous worship of the Persians, he became, so to speak, an incarnation of the world-power which in every generation opposes itself to the kingdom of God.

3. **Alexander and the Jews.**—Some interesting traditions have been handed down regarding this monarch's relations with the Jews. Josephus states that during his siege of Tyre he wrote to the Jewish high priest "to send him some auxiliaries, and to supply his army with provisions"; but only to get back the retort, that his oath of allegiance to the King of Persia forbade such a thing. Alexander vowed vengeance, and, after taking Tyre and Gaza, marched against Jerusalem. On reaching the eminence of Sapha, with both city and temple full in view, he was met by a strange procession streaming forth from the open gates. At its head was the high priest Jaddua in his pontifical robes ; beside him walked the priests in their linen garments ; the entire population, dressed in white, followed in the rear. Thus calmly the Jews awaited the approach of the conqueror. To the surprise of his followers, Alexander prostrated himself before the Jewish

leader, and adored the ineffable name inscribed upon his mitre.
Parmenio alone ventured to ask an explanation. " Why should
he whom all men worship, worship the high priest of the Jews?"
" Not him," replied the king, " but the God whose high priest he
is I worship. Long ago, when at Dium in Macedonia, I saw in
my dreams such an one in such an attire as this, who urged me
to undertake the conquest of Persia, and succeed." Amid an
escort of priests he then entered the city, and, under the direction
of the high priest, offered sacrifice to God in the temple. Shown
the prophecy of the overthrow of Persia by a Grecian, he at once
interpreted it in his own favour. As if in gratitude for this
unlooked for omen of success, Alexander granted the Jews
absolute religious liberty, and exempted them from taxation
every seventh year. On his also offering the like privileges to
those who would join his army, many elected to accompany him
in his wars. The story is probably legendary, but it may at least
be taken as evidence of Alexander's humane treatment of the
Jews. In exchanging the Persian dominion for the Greek they
certainly reaped no disadvantage.

4. The Diadochoi.—Alexander's death fell like a thunder-clap
upon the world, and many complications arose in connection
with the government of the empire. The half-witted Philip of
Aridæus was made interim king, and for seven years nominally
enjoyed the sovereign power, those who had distinguished themselves in the army being appointed military satraps over the
various provinces. But this proved an unworkable arrangement,
owing to the ambition of these satraps, who were anxious to
establish independent kingdoms for themselves. Some of them
aimed even at the imperial crown. Doubt has been thrown upon
the statement that "Alexander parted his kingdom among his
servants while yet he was alive" (1 Macc. i. 6) ; but, at anyrate,
they divided it among themselves after he was dead. Upon the
murder of Roxana and her boy of thirteen by Cassander in order
to secure himself in the possession of Macedonia, they made no

secret of their selfish designs. Ultimately, in B.C. 301, *five* kings shared the vast inheritance. These were Seleucus, the powerful lord of Babylon ; Antigonus, the ambitious ruler of Phrygia, and the ablest of the Diadochoi or Successors ; Ptolemy Lagi, who obtained Egypt ; Lysimachus, who had Thrace and Bithynia ; and Cassander, who reigned over Macedonia and Greece. But this partition did not bring peace to the world. Antigonus especially was not satisfied with his portion, and soon showed that he meant to seize the whole empire. Aided by his talented son Demetrius, he all but succeeded in his struggle for the mastery. But the generalship of Lysimachus and the countless hosts of Seleucus, together with his own senile impatience, turned the scale adversely for Antigonus. After a well-contested battle at Ipsus in Phrygia (B.C. 301), he was slain, and his troops laid down their arms. Demetrius fled with some thousands of men, and, by utilising his superior fleet, kept the world in commotion until he was taken captive by Seleucus. Only at the end of more than twenty years of warfare were the four generals in a position to divide the empire between them. Even then they were filled with mutual jealousies. Seleucus, Ptolemy, and Lysimachus kept a sharp eye upon each other's movements ; while Demetrius, on the death of Cassander, seated himself on the throne of Macedonia, and began to meditate a repetition of his father's tactics. Of these monarchs only Seleucus and Ptolemy play any part in the history of Israel. The former profited most by the battle of Ipsus. Ptolemy had put in a claim for Phœnicia and Syria, but, owing to his half-heartedness in the war, this territory fell to Seleucus, who now became lord of all the East. That Syria gave its name to his kingdom was due to the situation of Antioch, his capital, in the extreme west of his dominions. Ptolemy I. (Soter), besides retaining Egypt, obtained possession of Palestine and some other parts adjacent to the Mediterranean. From its situation between Syria and Egypt, Judea had the misfortune to be for more than a century the battlefield of these two powers, which are referred to in

Dan. xi. as the kingdoms of the north and south respectively. All the Diadochoi continued the Hellenising policy of the great Macedonian.

CHAPTER II

THE CONFLICT BETWEEN HELLENISM AND JUDAISM

The legend of Alexander overawed at the sight of the high priest is one very befitting the rise of the new era, in which we see Judaism in contact with the aggressive influences of the West. Two very different currents met at this time and mingled their waters, and the broad stream that was made up of the two tributaries flowed on in a subsequent course that would have been impossible apart from this union. Greek worldliness dashed up against Hebrew religion ; Greek freedom encountered Hebrew legalism ; Greek philosophy was met by Hebrew simplicity ; Greek radicalism was resisted by Hebrew conservatism. It was the shock of progress. Each had something to gain from the other. The blending of two such contrary forces proved rich in results for the whole world. The spiritual inheritance God had given could no longer be confined within the limits of a single race. Not only were the Hebrew Scriptures translated into Greek, but many Jews and Gentiles were living side by side, and exercising often an unconscious influence on one another's modes of thought and articles of belief. All this was providentially ordered. It was the divine preparation on the path of history for the advent of Him who is " the desire of all nations."

The time, then, was one of restless and revolutionary change. New cities were being built in Palestine by Greek enterprise, and increasing numbers of Jews, either from stress of circum-

stances or from their own choice, began to emigrate eastwards
as far as India, and westwards to Phœnicia and other countries.
The tide of Hellenism [1] swept over Jewish territory, while
Judaism, on the other hand, compensated itself by colonisation
all over the civilised world. Very far-reaching were the results
of these two simultaneous movements.

1. **The Diffusion of Hellenism.**—At this epoch the splendid
civilisation of Greece began to be sown broadcast over the
earth. Colonists from Miletus alone spread themselves in
numerous townships round the entire coast of the Black Sea.
Italy as well as Western Asia became the home of Greek arts
and sciences, of Greek philosophy and literature. Cities colonised
by Greeks sprang up everywhere in the wake of Alexander's
army. The movement asserted itself on Jewish soil as elsewhere. Pella and Dium on the east of Jordan ; Paneas and
Scythopolis in Galilee ; Anthedon on the coast, and Arethusa in
the interior, may be taken as typical examples of cities whose
names sufficiently attest their Greek origin. Judea was now the
only part of Palestine with a purely Jewish population, and it was
enclosed by a network of Greek cities. Of these, some were new,
built and inhabited exclusively by Greek colonists ; others were
simply restored, and contained a mixed population of Jews and
Greeks ; but all alike had become saturated with the Hellenistic
spirit. Native customs had everywhere retired before this great
assimilating force. The presence of the Greek civilian had
wrought more transformation than the invasion of the Greek
phalanx. The subtle leaven of Hellenism had entered into the
life of the various communities, and it had not been long at work
before the whole was leavened. Every department of life was
affected. The Greek mind stamped itself not only on education

---

[1] The term Hellenism does not point to racial descent ; it indicates rather
a certain bent of mind, type of character, and peculiarity of spirit. It may
be described as the subtle soul of Greece which asserted itself as a civilising
force in every sphere of life.

and learning, but also on religion and politics, on trade and fashion. Its attitude towards every kind of foreign culture was that of a plastic accommodation ; but, in return for this, it always constituted itself the ruling element. The most powerful influence in disseminating Greek ideas and customs was doubtless the world-wide adoption of the Greek tongue. It now became the universal language, much as Latin became the common language of learned Europe during the Middle Ages, and as French subsequently gained the position of *la langue universelle*. With the acquisition of the Greek speech the mixed races of the East imbibed almost necessarily the Greek spirit.

2. **Adherence of the Jews to their ancestral Faith.** — There was no apparent bar to the process of fusion between Greek and Hebrew. The larger culture of the one, and the stricter ethic of the other, were invaluable contributions towards the formation of a finer type of human life than had been reached by either of them separately ; and the union of these two elements must have presented to many minds an attractive picture. But this union could never take place on the Greek terms, which were that Judaism should consent practically to efface itself in favour of Hellenism. The Jews were still determined to adhere to their charter of nationality—the religion of their fathers ; and in Palestine the Greek influence made itself felt only very slowly. The establishment of Greek townships as missionary centres of Greek culture did not serve its purpose among the Jews as among other nationalities. They could live under a Greek constitution, and still refuse to be Grecised, and to this circumstance was due the bitter struggle which bulks as the central fact in the Israelitish history of the period. The gradual and persistent encroachment of the Greek ideal of life only served to bring into bolder relief the essentially antagonistic features of Judaism. How indomitable was the spirit of the latter the Greeks were to learn later on. Their philosophy and culture, so far from annihilating it, were but the chisels used to tone down the sharp corners of Judaism, and the instruments

in the hand of God for placing on a wider basis the essence of that truth which is eternal.

3. The Jewish Dispersion.—The term "Dispersion"[1] is used to denote all Jews living in foreign parts, and maintaining their distinctive religious testimony among the heathen. The area over which the Dispersion extended was largely increased by the Greek conquests in Asia. At least a century before our era there were Jewish inhabitants in every corner of the civilised world.[2] *Four* well-defined groups of non-Palestinian Jews are distinguishable : (1) Jews dwelling beyond the Euphrates. These were held in the highest repute by their brethren in Palestine, and had their headquarters in the cities of Nehardea and Nisibis. (2) Jews were very numerous also in Syria, especially in Antioch and Damascus. From Syria they penetrated into Asia Minor. Antiochus the Great planted 2000 loyal Jews in the rebellious regions of Lydia and Phrygia. They showed a marked preference, however, for Ephesus, Pergamos, Sardis, and other large commercial cities on the west coast. (3) But the greatest exodus was to Egypt. Many went there with Alexander's army, and settled in the new city called by his name. Under Ptolemy I. and his successor they formed about two-fifths of the whole population. In Philo's day they were reckoned to be about a million strong. From Egypt the tide of emigration flowed westwards along the African coast. In Cyrene the Jews numbered one-fourth of the inhabitants. (4) There was also "the Dispersion among the Greeks" (John vii. 35). At Thessalonica, Berea, Athens, and Corinth, St. Paul found his way to "the synagogue of the Jews." Cyprus, Crete, and the smaller islands of the Ægean were also favourite resorts of the Jews. Latterly, they formed a numerous community in Rome, lived in a locality of their own across the

---

[1] In Hebrew *Gâluth*, which means "stripped naked"; in Greek, *Diaspora*, which conveys the idea of seed sown with a view to harvest. Cf. John vii. 35; Jas. i. 1; 1 Pet. i. 1.

[2] Cf. Acts ii. 9-11.

Tiber, and played a considerable part in the history of the empire. The *civil* standing of the Jews throughout the Dispersion was not a fixed quantity. In Alexandria they had all the rights of citizenship. This was recognised by Israelites everywhere as the ideal position to be aimed at. Conscious of their religious superiority, they could afford to be content with political equality. And in many quarters they enjoyed this, as, *e.g.*, in Cyrene, Berenice (Tripolis), Sardis, Ephesus, as well as in Antioch and all towns founded by Seleucus I. Nicator. Under the Ptolemies and the Seleucidæ (with some exceptions), the Jews were everywhere treated with toleration ; under the Romans also, religious freedom and exemption from military service were conceded to them by law. In *social* standing the Jews naturally fell somewhat behind the dominant races of the various municipalities, but they sometimes filled influential and responsible public posts. In Egypt especially, under the Ptolemies, many of them held the highest offices, both civil and military.

The type of Judaism developed in the Dispersion differed considerably from that which obtained in Palestine. Influenced by its environment, it took on a colour of its own in accordance with the forces of Gentile culture with which it came in contact. Thus one type prevailed in Babylonia, and another in Egypt. The distinction between the Palestinian and the Babylonian Jew was, however, owing to the current Aramaic dialect, slight compared with that which marked off both from the cultured Jew of Alexandria. That city soon grew to be the acknowledged literary capital of the world. It was the meeting-place between Jew and Greek. On the soil of Alexandria first Judaism, and afterwards Christianity, encountered the subtle influences of Greek thought. And thus arose a process both of assimilation and of conflict which lasted for centuries before the true faith was able finally to declare itself the victor. The Alexandrian Jew was in reality both a Jew and a Greek ; he held the faith of Jehovah, and sincerely worshipped the God of his fathers ; but he spoke the Greek language, had received a Greek education, and had contracted many Greek ideas and habits. Still, those in this position were Jews first and Greeks afterwards, and on all the "fundamentals" were in thorough sympathy with their Palestinian brethren.

The relation of Judaism in the Dispersion to the central sanctuary was wonderfully close and well maintained. Two things in particular served to keep up the connection—the sending of the temple dues payable by every male Israelite over twenty years of age, and the custom of making pilgrimages to the holy city at the feasts. Notwithstanding the Dispersion, the heart of the nation continued to beat in Jerusalem, which thus became to the Jewish what Rome has long been to the Latin Church, and Mecca to the Muslims.

Another feature about the Judaism of the Dispersion was that bound up with the name "proselytes." Under this designation were included those of the heathen who had more or less completely attached themselves to Mosaism (Neh. x. 28), and whom the prophetic vision pictured as flocking to the Lord's house from the four winds of heaven to share the inheritance of the tribes of Israel.[1] The spread of Jewish principles became a matter of first-rate importance in view of the realisation of these hopes, and under the Greek and Roman supremacy the claims of Judaism were vigorously pushed, not only by the Alexandrian Jews, but by the Palestinian Pharisees, who "compassed sea and land to make one proselyte." In apostolic times, the "proselytes" constituted an important link between Jewish and Gentile Christians. Theoretically they were entitled to equal privileges with the lineal sons of Abraham, but they were never held in quite the same esteem. Their position was very much like that accorded to converted Jews by Christian communities in the present day.

4. The Septuagint.—As the Jews who had migrated to Alexandria and other parts had exchanged their mother tongue for the Greek, a translation of the Old Testament into that language became a religious necessity. This is the most natural explana-

---

[1] Mic. iv. 1, 2; Isa. ii. 2, 3; Ezek. xlvii. 22.

tion of the origin of the Alexandrian version, although it probably derives the title of *Septuagint* or LXX. from a legend ascribing its production to seventy (or more precisely, seventy-two) translators drafted from Jerusalem by the literary zeal of the Egyptians. The story, as given in the letter of Aristeas, and adopted by Josephus, is as follows : Demetrius Phalereus, librarian at Alexandria under Ptolemy II. Philadelphus (B.C. 284-247), suggested the desirability of enriching the royal collection with a Greek translation of the Jewish law. The king despatched the captain of his guard and Aristeas to Jerusalem, with rich gifts for Eleazar the high priest, and with the request that he would, from each of the twelve tribes, send six elderly men of character, learning, and ability to undertake the work. Eleazar sent the seventy-two scholars with a copy of the law, which he asked should be returned after it had been translated. Arrived at Alexandria, the Jewish deputies were feasted for seven days at the king's table, and answered his questions in such a way as to fill him with admiration for their wisdom. Thereafter a quiet retreat was provided for them on the island of Pharos. Each day they set to work independently upon a certain portion of the Pentateuch, and then by comparing notes agreed upon a harmonious version, which was written down by Demetrius. The whole was thus overtaken in seventy-two days. The translation was then read to the Jewish residents, who formally accepted it as a faithful and final interpretation of the law.

Whatever be the truth as to its origin, it is clear from the linguistic peculiarities of the Septuagint itself that we do not owe it to the scholars of Palestine.[1] On the other hand, everything points to the conclusion that the new version was prepared at Alexandria ; that the work was begun in the reign of Ptolemy II.; and that the Pentateuch was translated first.[2] The completion

[1] "Sive regis jussu, sive sponte a Judæis, a Judæis Alexandrinis fuisse factam."—Hody.

[2] "The translation of the law is advantageously distinguished above that of the majority of the other books by its fidelity, intelligibility, and uniformity." —Ewald, *History*, v. p. 251

of the Greek Bible by different hands was only a matter of time. It is impossible to fix the precise dates at which the several books were rendered; but the *Prophets* must have taken precedence of the *Hagiographa*, some of which were not written till a comparatively late date. From the prologue to Ecclesiasticus, it appears that by the middle of the second century B.C. the whole of the Old Testament had been translated into Greek.

The new version was everywhere adopted by the Hellenistic Jews, and soon won for itself in popular esteem a place hardly second to that of the Hebrew original itself. It was through the LXX. that the Old Testament became the property of the whole world. Even in Palestine the story of its origin appears to have found acceptance, and no question was raised as to its inspiration. Josephus makes more use of it than of the Hebrew text. It was only when it began to be employed as a weapon against them in the great controversy with Christianity, that the Jews assumed a contemptuous attitude towards it, and showed a marked preference for other versions.

5. The Jewish-Alexandrian Philosophy.—After the translation of the Scriptures, foreign influences swept in upon Judaism like a flood. It became common for the colonial Jew to take a Greek *alias*; and Greek customs were accepted as freely as Greek names. Jews remained Jews, however—at least outwardly—wherever they went. In the mental and spiritual exchange which took place at this epoch the men of the East gave as much as they received. If the Greeks contributed their philosophy, the Orientals contributed their religion. We see in the Jewish-Alexandrian philosophy the historical form in which was blended the spirit of both races. The elaboration of the structure was due to the philosophical acumen of the Greeks; whatever soul there was in it was implanted by Judaism. But if the Alexandrian Jews had still old roots binding them to Jerusalem, there were also new roots ever more firmly attaching them to Alexandria. Here the most powerful forces at work in the world—Greek,

Oriental, Egyptian—met in mutual action, and gave new direction and impulse to the thought of the age.   In the time of the Ptolemies, Alexandria was at once the centre of the world's industry and commerce, the seat of regal magnificence and Oriental luxury, and the metropolis of Hellenic art and science.   The better minds among the Jews could not remain insensible to the charms of this rich and throbbing life.   They became philosophers, designating themselves by one or other of the distinctive names applied to the existing schools of Greek philosophy.   In doing this they had no intention of renouncing their ancient faith. What they did was rather to make use of the new methods which philosophy supplied for its defence and propagation.   All this, however, tended to the putting of pagan wisdom on a level with revealed wisdom, and afterwards resulted in desperate efforts to bring about a final adjustment between philosophy and Judaism.

The influence of Alexandrian thought is already traceable in the pages of the Septuagint, particularly in connection with such passages as speak in an anthropomorphic way about Jehovah.[1] In the oldest as well as in the more recent portions of this version these are very much toned down.   The same tendency is still more marked in the Greek Apocrypha of the Old Testament, in parts of which the spiritual nature of God is apprehended in a remarkable degree.[2]   Specially worthy of note in this connection is the *Wisdom of Solomon*, one of the finest products of the Alexandrian school, and presenting their philosophy in a somewhat developed form.   The Jewish *Sibyllines*, too, collected in the latter half of the second century B.C.,

---

[1] Compare Dante's lines—
> "From things sensible alone ye learn
> That, which, digested rightly, after turns
> To intellectual.   For no other cause
> The Scripture, condescending graciously
> To your perception, hands and feet to God
> Attributes, nor so means."
> —*Paradise*, iv. 41-46.

[2] See Ecclus. xliii. 31, 32 ; Wisd. i. 7, ix. 17, xiii. 1.

exhibit many of the characteristics of Hellenistic thought. But there was also a corresponding attempt to introduce Hebrew theology into Greek literature. A little tinkering of the original text, together with the desire to read the truths of revelation into well-known pagan works, produced sometimes astonishing results. The doctrine of the world's creation in six days and the Sabbath-rest upon the seventh was found in the *Odyssey*, while Sophocles was brought under contribution as an exponent of the unity of God. Many writers dealt also with sacred themes in the style of the recognised masters of the poetic art.

It was in connection with the Alexandrian speculation that the habit of allegorising the Old Testament Scriptures came into fashion. These philosophers discarded the literal meaning as vulgar, misleading, and insufficient. With the object of wedding philosophy to religion, they got into the way of using the sacred writings as a peg on which to hang their own ideas—a purpose which, from their antiquity and authority, they were excellently fitted to serve. But the absurdities of interpretation into which they were thus led were equal to, if not greater than, those which on other lines were indulged in by the Rabbis of Palestine. In the hands of such men the Bible could be made to mean anything or nothing. The first well-known Jewish author devoting himself to this kind of work was Aristobulus, who lived at Alexandria under Ptolemy Philometor (B.C. 180–146). He was held in great honour at Court, and is described by the Fathers as an Aristotelian. The task to which he addressed himself was that of harmonising the early Greek philosophy with the record of revelation, from which he alleged it had been borrowed. The allegorical style reached its height in the works of Philo, a century and a half later. So long as it prevailed, the support of Scripture could be claimed for speculations of the most *outré* description. It was to the detriment of Judaism that it was thus dropped into the crucible of Hellenistic philosophy ; and the consequences were not less disastrous when the Platonic method was afterwards applied to Christianity. There may be a philosophy of religion legitimate enough ; but it can never be legitimate to apply philosophical methods to Bible statements with the design of conserving certain philosophical views, *i.e.* until we are prepared to discard all authority and make reason supreme.

6. Hellenism in Judea.—The necessities of trade compelled the Jew to have intercourse with the Gentile. This could be had only through the medium of the universal language. But as they gained fluency in the Greek tongue, many Jews began to adopt the Greek customs. This was especially the case with the educated and upper classes. Attracted by the glitter of the Greek life, they began to covet Greek liberty. As they were introduced to Greek art, their sense of beauty was awakened and developed. There seemed to open before their astonished gaze a new world of whose existence they had scarcely dreamed. The spectacular displays of the amphitheatre, the allurements of the gymnasium, the orgies of the Bacchanalian festival, completely intoxicated them. Some renounced Judaism altogether ; others, more sober-minded, wished merely to avail themselves of the advantages and pleasures of Greek life without otherwise giving up religion. Under the Seleucidæ matters became worse ; the magic spell of Hellenism had at length fairly fallen upon Judea.

Simultaneously, however, with the influx of Greek culture, there had been, owing to the labours of the scribes, a great perfecting of legalistic Judaism. The two systems were essentially antagonistic, and the war-cry had sooner or later to be raised. Accordingly, the movement in the direction of Hellenism was counteracted by another in favour of the utmost rigour in carrying out the precepts of the law. Those who identified themselves with the latter were known as "the pious." Perceiving that the Greek civilisation was as inwardly rotten as it was outwardly fascinating, they strove to live in the undisturbed practice of their laws and customs, and to follow out the ideal set before them by the scribes. Besides this unwearied study of the law, there were in the national life of Judea other elements of permanence with which Hellenism had to reckon. To the worthier section of the community the inheritance of their past history was very precious, while the unfailing observance of the temple worship continued also to give strength and purpose to Hebrew sentiment. Yet it could not roll back the wave of pagan civilisation ; all it could do was to offer it a successful resistance on its *religious* side. The heathen worship was kept out of Judea ; but in all other depart- ments of life the Hellenistic spirit continued to make headway. A majority of the people, indeed, appear to have been more or less in sympathy with the Greek party, when the madness of Antiochus Epiphanes came to the aid of "the pious." His attempt to abolish Judaism, root and branch, caused the Maccabean revolt, and ended in the banishment from Jewish territory of everything that savoured of Hellenism, at all events in the sphere of religion. Ere the dawn of the Roman period, however, it had again to a considerable extent overrun the Holy Land.

CHAPTER III

THE GREEK DOMINION

1. **The Ptolemies.**—The Ptolemaic dynasty was founded by Ptolemy Lagi, the far-seeing general to whom Egypt was allotted upon the division of Alexander's empire. The campaigns in which he had to fight Antigonus for the possession of Phœnicia and Cœle-Syria, form the first of a long series of wars between the Egyptian and Syrian powers. In B.C. 320, on a Sabbath day, he took Jerusalem ; but five years later he had to retire before Antigonus. After several changes in the balance of power, the battle of Ipsus left him in possession of Palestine, which for a century thereafter remained an appanage of the Egyptian crown.

Although for twenty years involved in warfare, Ptolemy's own decided preferences lay in the direction of cultivating the arts of peace. If he did not himself found the famous museum and library of Alexandria, he at all events collected the materials.

After having reigned for thirty-eight years, Ptolemy Soter handed over his kingdom to his youngest son, Philadelphus (B.C. 284-247). The latter, being in weak health, did not conduct the Syrian campaign, but (fortunately for Palestine) commissioned his allies in Greece and Asia Minor to carry on the war. While prepared to defend his kingdom by the sword, Ptolemy Philadelphus sought other means of strengthening it. He did much for learning and commerce. His collection of books, statues, and pictures was such as no prince had ever yet possessed. Under his benign influence there took place a revival of letters which reacted in several important respects upon Judaism. In the Alexandrian school, criticism bulked more largely than independent thought; but through the prevailing eclecticism of the age Jew and Gentile were brought more into line intellectually, and for the first time found it possible to understand each other.

With Philadelphus disappeared "the last representative of the old Greek 'tyrannos' whom Pindar has made known to us"; the next emperor, Ptolemy III. Euergetes (B.C. 247-222), resembled more one of the fighting "Diadochoi." The war between Philadelphus and Antiochus Theos had been terminated by a marriage-treaty, in terms of which the Syrian monarch divorced his wife Laodice, and married Berenice, the daughter of Ptolemy. But on the death of Philadelphus the situation was reversed by the expulsion of Berenice, and the reinstatement of Laodice as queen. The latter, to prevent another change, poisoned her fickle husband, caused her rival, along with her son and all the Egyptian retinue, to be slain, and placed the crown upon her own son, Seleucus Callinicus. To avenge his sister's death, Ptolemy cut off Laodice, and brought the kingdom of Syria to the verge of destruction. The remainder of his reign was principally devoted to the extension of his empire. Euergetes was not, however, a mere soldier. He inherited the literary instincts of his predecessors, and their considerateness towards the Jews. On his return from Syria he showed his goodwill by "offering sacrifices in the temple at Jerusalem, and adding gifts worthy of his victory." Some time afterwards, however, the imprudence of the high priest Onias II. came near to causing a rupture with Egypt. Apparently an adherent of the Syrian party, and now a surly old man, he obstinately kept back the usual tribute-money. Ptolemy threatened summary measures, and everything pointed to a crisis. But through the exceptional address shown by the high priest's ambitious nephew, Joseph the son of Tobias, who approached in person the angry king, the matter was amicably settled. Not only so ; Joseph's wit, affability, and open-handedness made him a *persona grata* at the Egyptian Court, and he secured the coveted post of receiver-general of taxes for the whole of Palestine.

The century covered by the reigns of the first three Ptolemies forms the golden age of the Jews in Egypt, and was also for their Palestinian brethren a period of comparative quiet, prosperity, and happiness. Things altered very much under the son and successor of Euergetes, the voluptuous and indolent Ptolemy Philopator (B.C. 221-204). Irritated that an Egyptian garrison should have been quartered in Seleucia, Antiochus (III.) the Great, king of Syria, attempted to seize upon Palestine and Cœle-Syria. Ptolemy was forced at length to take action, and defeated Antiochus at Raphia, near Gaza, in B.C. 217. The disputed territory was recovered as a condition of peace, and Ptolemy signalised his victory by a tour through the Eastern provinces. In due course he arrived, it is said, at Jerusalem, offered sacrifices of thanksgiving, and bestowed rich gifts on the temple. As he was on the point of forcing his way into the inner sanctuary, however, he was struck down with paralysis. On his return to Alexandria he disfranchised and persecuted the Egyptian Jews, and even meditated the extermination of the whole nation. This narrative (in 3 Macc.) may contain a historical germ ; Ptolemy may have treated the Jews with great barbarity. The Jews, moreover, had hitherto enjoyed the protection of the Court, but no sooner was this withdrawn than they found themselves between two fires. Their Greek neighbours envied their material prosperity, and the native Egyptians could ill brook that privileges denied to themselves should have been conferred upon an alien race.

Because the slothful Philopator did not follow up his victory over Antiochus, there was rebellion in Egypt. This first revolt of the natives against their Greek masters was, however, successfully overcome, and thereafter Ptolemy abandoned himself to vice. He died in B.C. 204, and was succeeded by his infant son, Ptolemy V. Epiphanes (204-181). The kings of Macedonia and Syria at once made a combined effort to wrest from Egypt and divide between themselves the outlying provinces of that empire. Antiochus successfully invaded Palestine, and, finding that the Jews, whether owing to the cruelty of Philopator, or from utilitarian motives, were largely on his side, he showed his appreciation of their friendly attitude by lavishing favours alike on the temple and the city. Not long afterwards, however, the Egyptian general Scopas succeeded in placing a garrison in Jerusalem. But in B.C. 198, Antiochus more than retrieved this disaster by inflicting on him a heavy defeat at Paneas, in the valley of the Jordan. Antiochus would fain have invaded Egypt itself, but an intimation from the Romans that they had taken the young Ptolemy under their guardianship caused him to desist. In these circumstances Antiochus proposed that his daughter Cleopatra should wed the young Egyptian king, and promised Cœle-Syria, Phœnicia, and Palestine as her dowry, on condition that the revenues should be shared equally by the two kings. This offer was accepted, and peace concluded. The goal which the Syrian monarchs had long been striving to reach was now attained, and Palestine was merged in the kingdom of the Seleucidæ.

2. **The Book of Ecclesiasticus.**—Towards the close of this period was written, in Hebrew,[1] the important work to which the Latin Church has given the name of Ecclesiasticus (*liber*, *i.e.* a book for the use of the Church), but which is better characterised by its Greek title, "The Wisdom of Jesus the Son of Sirach."[2] The form in which we possess it is that of the translation into Greek by the grandson of Jesus, executed in Egypt in B.C. 132. We may therefore conjecture that the original work was composed within the decade B.C. 190-180. A high value was attached to this book, not only by the Rabbis, but by the early Christian Fathers, who freely cite it as Holy Scripture.

The style of writing is akin to that of Proverbs and Ecclesiastes. The book is a further development on the same lines, and a contribution to the Hebrew *Hochmah* or *Wisdom*. If the Hebrews can be said to have had a philosophy at all, it was that embodied in proverbs, and in the later ages of Jewish history this species of writing was much in vogue. As in Proverbs, it is the relation of God to the individual that occupies the mind of the writer ; but there is more connection in this book, and a more extended handling of distinct topics.

The ruling conception is that of wisdom. To be wise is to have found out the secret of a God-pleasing and happy life. The author seeks to help all who desire to lead such a life. His book is essentially practical in its aim, and sets forth the results of thought and study, observation and experience, as the true basis of conduct. As a devout Jew he ascribes wisdom to a divine source. The Almighty, in whom this attribute of wisdom has resided from eternity, has revealed it to men through the medium of the Jewish law. The book exhorts to fulfilment of the law as a whole : there is no detailed exposition of single commandments after the manner of the later Scribism. On the other hand, we

---

[1] Jerome mentions having seen a Hebrew text.

[2] Of his personal history nothing is known. The statement that he was a high priest (Syncellus) is groundless. It is much more likely that he was a scribe. Cf. chap. li. 23-25.

have an exceedingly detailed treatment of the various relation-
ships of life from the standpoint of the truly wise. The author
practically sets himself to answer the question, Given a particular
case affecting any condition of life or class of persons, what is
the proper course for the wise man to take? The book is a
manual of conduct, and meant to be to the seeker after wisdom
what his ready-reckoner and his tables of interest are to the
trader. Rules are laid down directing one how to act in all
emergencies of individual, social, commercial, religious, and
domestic life. If occasional tendencies to coarseness of language, false teaching, and worldly prudence mark it off from
the loftier tone of the canonical writings, by far the greater
portion of this long work of fifty-one chapters is distinguished by
remarkable elevation and spirituality. Quite an original feature
is the long eulogium on the historical heroes of Israel's past.
The writer to the Hebrews no doubt took the idea of his eleventh
chapter from Ecclesiasticus. This interesting book is not only
the greatest monument of the Palestinian Judaism, but also the
brightest and fullest reflection of the manners and customs of the
age that produced it.

3. **The Seleucidæ.**—One result attending their new conditions
was that the Israelitish nation was swept into the current of
general history, and had given to it a visibility which it never
could have possessed as part of the geographically detached
kingdom of Egypt. Jewish expectations were again, however,
doomed to disappointment. Owing to the incessant wars between Syria and Egypt, the political position of their country
lacked stability, and tended to create a distaste for the Greek
dominion in any form. There was, indeed, between it and the
spirit of Judaism an essential contradiction, which was becoming
daily more apparent. In point of fact, the Jews had now entered
on one of the darkest eras of their history. Antiochus might
have continued to befriend them, but his own difficulties rendered
this impossible. The Romans were easily persuaded by some

Greek cities in Asia Minor to interfere with the ambitious designs
of the Syrian monarch, who declined, however, to listen to their
ambassadors.   In B.C. 195, Hannibal, having reason to flee from
Carthage, joined Antiochus, and advised him to invade Italy as
the only way of vanquishing the Romans.   What between sus-
pecting Hannibal and wasting his strength in a fruitless expedition into Greece, the Syrian king lost the opportunity of his life.
The Romans surprised and defeated him at Thermopylæ.
Hastily retreating beyond the Hellespont, he next tried his
fortune at sea, but the losses of his fleet proved to be greater
than their gains.   Finally, in B.C. 190, his army was utterly
routed at Magnesia.   The terms of peace were that he should
cede all territory west of Mount Taurus, and pay the entire cost
of the war in twelve yearly instalments.   His son Antiochus was
also sent to Rome, along with other hostages, in security for the
payment of the money.   Henceforth the Syrian kings were little
more than tax-gatherers for the Romans.   Compelled to replenish
their empty exchequer, they adopted the desperate policy of
plundering temples within their own dominions.   It was while
engaged upon an expedition of this sort at Elymais that Antiochus
met his death in B.C. 187.

Under his son, Seleucus IV. Philopator (187–176), the Syrian
kingdom continued to suffer from chronic impecuniosity.   In his
straits Seleucus was only too ready to welcome any means of
obtaining money.   An opportunity soon arose.   A priest named
Simon, a Benjamite, and governor of the temple at Jerusalem,
had quarrelled with the high priest, Onias III.   Out of spite
against Onias, and in the hope that, with the help of the Syrian
king, he would himself be promoted to the high priesthood, this
"son of Tobias" went to Apollonius, then governor of Cœle-
Syria, and advised him to despoil the temple of what he alleged
to be its vast and superfluous treasures.   Seleucus sent Heliodorus
his treasurer with an order to seize " the foresaid money " (2 Macc.
iii. 4–7).   Heliodorus is said to have been deterred from entering
the sanctuary only by a miraculous apparition from heaven.

"By the hand of God he was cast down and lay speechless"; but through the prayers of Onias his life was spared. Meanwhile Simon was furthering his designs at the Court of Syria, where he diligently "slandered Onias," and maintained that the mission of Heliodorus had failed owing to the trickery of the high priest. As these proceedings at Antioch were simultaneous with certain outrages committed by "one of Simon's faction in Jerusalem," Onias thought fit to visit the Syrian Court in person. Ere he was ready to leave the banks of the Orontes, Seleucus was poisoned by the dastardly hand of Heliodorus. The latter hoped to obtain the crown for himself, the true heir, Demetrius, having just been sent to Rome as a hostage in room of Antiochus, the younger brother of Seleucus, who had not yet returned to Syria. But this project did not succeed. An adroit appeal to Eumenes, king of Pergamus, enabled Antiochus on his return to displace Heliodorus and peaceably to usurp the kingdom.

On his accession, Antiochus IV. assumed the title of Epiphanes (the Illustrious), but this soon gave way to the nickname Epimanes (the Madman). He is alluded to in Dan. xi. 21 as "a vile person," and he lived to justify the description. According to Polybius, he was characterised by a strong individuality, in which the prominent features were a fondness for display, a tendency to indulge in various kinds of tomfoolery with low-class people, and an erratic but kingly munificence. His relations to the Jews, however, were marked less by an absurd eccentricity than by brutal and savage cruelty. Hitherto they had fared at least as well under the Syrian rule as they had done at the hands of the Ptolemies, and had once and again received gifts for the temple. All this was now to be changed. Antiochus seems to have formed the idea of a dominant State religion as the best means of giving unity to the empire. Hence his ill-starred attempt to compel the universal adoption of the Greek polytheism. A section of the Jewish people were not only prepared to acquiesce in his plans, but to give them their active support, and in return for this he was disposed to let them have the upper hand in

Judea.   But these apostates misled Antiochus when they represented to him that the country was ripe for Hellenisation.   A
strenuous opposition was offered, and this engendered in the
mind of Antiochus a particular antipathy to the Jewish religion,
and a deep-seated hatred to the entire Jewish nation.   The
temple was plundered and desecrated ; every sort of violence
was used to suppress the observances of Judaism ; and the
adoption of Greek manners and customs was ruthlessly enforced.
Matters were thus brought to a crisis.   It soon became evident
that Antiochus could secure his end only by exterminating the
Jewish race.   Goaded at length into open rebellion, they took up
arms in the name of Jehovah, and fought for their lives and
their religious liberty.   Although this reign lasted but eleven
years (175–164), the stirring events by which it was marked make
it for Jewish history by far the most important in the dynasty of
the Seleucidæ.

4. Farming of the High Priesthood.—The high priest was still
the centre of power in Israel.   From the time of the Ptolemies,
however, an aristocratic Council of Elders assisted him in the
administration.   This court was called the *Gerousia*, and appears
to have been either constituted or reorganised under the reform-
ing influence of Hellenism.   Subsequently it developed into the
Sanhedrin.   In the roll of the high priesthood from the time of
Alexander to that of the Maccabees there are three names of
outstanding merit.   Simon the Just, grandson of Jaddua, was
distinguished for his piety, for his kindliness, and for his scholar-
ship.   Simon II., who showed the greatest enterprise in fortifying
the temple and city of Jerusalem, ministered also very nobly to
the spiritual necessities of the nation.[1]   In Onias III. we see a
godly man traduced by sordid relatives and victimised by cruel
circumstances.   He made a mistake in going to the Syrian Court,
where his lofty character counted for little so long as he main-

---

[1] The glowing tribute paid to him by the Son of Sirach (l. 1–21) is a highly
characteristic specimen of the style of the period.

tained the sacredness of the temple treasures, stood out for the observance of the Jewish rites, and opposed the spread of the Greek culture. Epiphanes at once accepted the proffered co-operation of the Greek party in Judea. This party was led by Joshua, a younger brother of the high priest, who had given one proof of his fitness for the position, by discarding his Hebrew name and calling himself, as a Hellenist, Jason. He offered to pay yearly to Antiochus 440 talents, provided he would depose Onias from the priesthood and confer it on himself ; with an additional sum of 150 talents should the king authorise him to set up a gymnasium at Jerusalem, and an Ephebeion or place for training the youth in the practice of Greek games and sports, and also to sell the burgess rights of Antioch to dwellers in the Holy City. Antiochus was naturally willing to agree to these proposals ; they suited his policy, and were advantageous to his purse. Onias was detained in Antioch so as to rid the pagan propaganda in Judea of its most powerful adversary ; the base supplanter of his brother, on the other hand, proved himself an energetic apostle of heathen customs and ways. Under the very citadel of Zion a gymnasium was erected ; multitudes donned the Greek dress ; even the priests neglected their duties in the temple to play at Discus (2 Macc. iv. 11–14). Laughed at by their Greek antagonists in the palæstra, the Jewish youths did their best to remove from their bodies the sign of the covenant (1 Macc. i. 15). So much had Jason already been able to effect ; but his most shameless action was still to come. Several Jews, whom he had made citizens of Antioch, were despatched by him to witness the Quinquennial games in honour of the Phœnician Hercules at Tyre, and with a contribution towards the expenses of the sacrifices offered to the heathen deity. They shrank from this impiety, however, and handed over the money for behoof of the navy. When, in preparing for a war with Egypt, Antiochus visited Jerusalem, he was received with every mark of honour. In all this Jason did not mean deliberately to renounce Judaism : he only desired to be a Jew in Hellenistic style, and to conform to

the pagan practice of respecting not only the native religion but
other religions as well. The Jews had foreign princes sacrificing
to Jehovah in Jerusalem ; why should they not send an offering
to Hercules in Tyre? In the eyes of devout sons of Israel the
two things were entirely different. The true God might be
glorified by offerings from any quarter, but it never could be
right for a son of Abraham to present gifts to the gods of
heathendom. To do so, with Jason and his company, were to
"revolt from the holy land and kingdom" (2 Macc. i. 7).

After three years' tenure of office (B.C. 174-171), Jason was in
his turn supplanted by Menelaus, a Hellenistic Jew of the
tribe of Benjamin, and brother of that Simon who had first
recommended the spoliation of the temple. By outbidding
Jason to the extent of 300 talents, he secured for himself the high
priesthood. Things had indeed reached a sad pass in Israel when
this sacred office could be sold to the highest bidder by a heathen
king. But Menelaus, although armed with the royal rescript, did
not easily dispossess Jason, who was supported by the mass of
the people. As a member of the Tobias party, the newly-appointed
high priest had no religious ideals, and he now shamelessly
announced his entire apostasy from Judaism. This led Antiochus
to give him military support, and Jason was obliged to retreat
across the Jordan. Menelaus, however, had another tough problem on hand in the shape of his debts. He was unable to pay
the heavy tribute he had promised, and for a time managed to
tide over his difficulties only by plundering the temple. Being
upbraided for this sacrilege by the exiled Onias III., he bribed
Andronicus, whom the king had left in charge at Antioch during
his absence, to murder that "prince of the covenant."[1] Lysimachus,
his brother, had meanwhile acted for Menelaus, and had contrived
to supply his needs by repeated raids upon the temple treasury.
On ascertaining this the people were furious ; 3000 armed men
were routed by them, while " as for the church robber himself, him
they slew beside the treasury." Three delegates from the Jewish

[1] Dan. xi. 22.

Gerousia appeared before the king at Tyre to impeach Menelaus for sacrilege. By resorting to bribery, this unprincipled scoundrel once more got his own way, while his righteous accusers, to the disgust of the Tyrians, were led forth to execution.

Jason had meanwhile been anxious to regain the priesthood ; but as long as Epiphanes favoured Menelaus this was hopeless. During the king's second expedition into Egypt, however, a false rumour of his death obtained currency in Palestine. At the head of a thousand men Jason suddenly bore down upon Jerusalem, and forced Menelaus to secure himself in the castle. Jason's position would have been difficult even had Antiochus been really dead, but with the despot already hastening from Egypt to punish a Jewish revolt, it became impossible. Driven again into exile, he died at length in Lacedæmon.

5. **Desecration of the Temple : Religious Persecution of the Jews : Formation of the Party of the Assideans.**—In B.C. 170, Antiochus arrived at Jerusalem, and, being told that the news of his death had been received there with joy, he ordered his troops to fall upon the ill-fated city. In three days 40,000 Jews were massacred, and as many were afterwards sold into slavery. Proceeding to the temple, with the traitorous Menelaus for his guide, he rifled it of all the valuables that it still contained, haughtily entered the Holy of Holies, and carried the sacred vessels to Antioch.

A still more dreadful experience awaited the sorrow-stricken community at Jerusalem. In B.C. 168, Antiochus set out on his last Egyptian campaign. Just as he was ready to grasp his prize, and stood once more within sight of Alexandria, Popilius Lænas, the ambassador of the Imperial Senate, suddenly appeared, and charged him, if he valued the friendship of the Romans, to abandon all hostile measures against Egypt. Antiochus evasively said he would consider the matter. But the proud Roman, drawing a circle round him with his staff, ordered him to make his decision before he moved from the spot. Brought thus to bay, Antiochus prudently promised to respect the Roman demand.

Thwarted in his schemes against Egypt, the tyrant determined to stamp out once for all the Jewish religion in Palestine. Accordingly, in B.C. 168–167, he sent Apollonius against Jerusalem with 22,000 men. Waiting for a Sabbath, "that detestable ringleader" fell upon the defenceless city, slew many of the people, and sold multitudes of women and children as slaves. After being looted, the city was set on fire ; the houses and walls also were demolished, and the sanctuary laid waste. All who could made their escape. Many fled to Egypt ; others hid themselves in caves or desert wilds. Strangers, on the other hand, were drafted in as colonists ; and as Menelaus and his adherents remained in possession, there was for the time an approximation to the ideal cherished by Antiochus. Jerusalem wore the aspect of a pagan city, and a Syrian garrison was placed in Acra.

But these were merely preliminary measures. Apollonius had been commissioned to destroy Judaism and establish paganism by force. Although this man's zeal needed no stimulus, Epiphanes issued an edict enjoining religious uniformity all over his kingdom, and wrote specially to the Jews, forbidding them on pain of death to observe their own religious rites. The Mosaic worship was now a thing of the past ; temple sacrifices, Sabbath observance, and circumcision were but Jewish reminiscences. No one was allowed to read or possess a copy of the Law. So far the negative side of the unholy programme. Its positive provisions were equally vile. The temple at Jerusalem was dedicated to Jupiter Olympius, and became the scene of licentious heathen orgies. In all the cities of Judea altars were erected, at which the Jews were forced to offer to pagan deities animals which to them were unclean, and then to eat of what had thus been sacrificed to idols. When the festival of Bacchus came round, they were compelled to join the public procession in honour of that deity. But the crowning profanation took place when, on the 25th day of Chisleu, B.C. 168, the first heathen sacrifice was offered upon an altar erected over the great altar of burnt-offering, and facing a statue of Jupiter. This is the "abomination of desolation" referred to in the Book of Daniel, and marks the height of the terrible religious persecution, which had its roots partly in the impecuniosity of the Syrian monarch, and partly in the unpatriotic mercenariness of many Hellenistic Jews. Antiochus appointed officers to see that his commands were enforced throughout the land. A monthly inquisition was held, and whoever was found to have concealed a copy of the Law, or to have had a child circumcised, or refused to eat unclean meats, was put to death. At the instance of one Ptolemy, these regulations were extended to the heathen cities around, so that it was nowhere " lawful for a man to keep Sabbath days or ancient feasts, or to profess himself at all to be a Jew."

Many were, of course, content to conform to Gentile customs in order to save their lives ; but the flower of Israel, the energetic men and women who loved their country, were prepared to die rather than renounce their faith. And these were in the majority. The details given in 2 Macc. about the tortures endured by Eleazar, an aged man of ninety, and about the cruel martyrdom of seven brothers and their mother in succession, for refusing to eat swine's flesh, may be more or less coloured, but they go to establish the fact that a large section of the people still clung to the religion of their fathers. Nothing sifts a nation like persecution ; it forces every man to take his side. Those who continued faithful to the law now entered into a solemn league to maintain their sacred institutions. Known at first by the name of the *Chasidîm*, or pious ones, and afterwards by that of Pharisees, they soon embraced within their party all that was bravest and best in Israel. Their action had no political significance : the one thing for which they contended was liberty to worship God according to their conscience. So extreme was their regard for the strict letter of the law, that as many as a thousand of them permitted themselves to be butchered by the Syrian soldiers rather than do anything in self-defence on the Sabbath day. But, with all their reluctance to take up arms, these pious men—the Covenanters of that age— soon perceived that they must choose between this and extermination. And so at last, along with all who were like-minded, they took the sword, and "smote sinful men in their anger, and wicked men in their wrath."

6. **Literature of the Persecution-time.**—A vivid picture of the havoc wrought by the enemy, and of the spirit shown by the people under the persecution of Antiochus, is supplied by certain psalms in the Psalter. Although most of the later psalms belong to the Persian period, it is certain that our collection contains psalms composed during the Greek supremacy also, some of these being undoubtedly Maccabean. There appears, indeed, to be a growing disposition on the part of Old Testament scholars to assign to this late date a considerable part of the whole collection. The objection that the Canon had been already closed, and that the theory of Maccabean psalms is therefore precluded, will satisfy no one. The real question is not as to the possibility, but as to the number, of such psalms. In our own country this subject has recently been lifted into prominence through the publication of Professor Cheyne's *Bampton Lectures* for 1889. Although we may not be able to accept all the conclusions of this writer, the perusal of his book must deepen the conviction that, if we could only date more of the psalms with certainty, the history of the post-Exilic period might be written as it has never yet been done. Unfortunately, it is too much ever to expect substantial agreement among critics with regard to the date of a good many psalms having no definite historical background; and in point of fact there has hitherto been the greatest diversity of opinion as to the number of psalms entitled to be considered as Maccabean. To this period Calvin ascribes 2, Theodore [1] 17, Cheyne 27, and Reuss as many as 38 psalms. Hitzig and Olshausen are even more sweeping. There are, however, at least *four*, the Maccabean origin of which has been very

---

[1] Bishop of Mopsuestia in Cilicia (*ob.* A.D. 429). He was the friend and fellow-student of Chrysostom, and the renowned "Interpreter" of the Syrian Church.

generally admitted, viz. Psalms xliv., lxxiv., lxxix., and lxxxiii. The internal grounds for ascribing them to this time of persecution are exceedingly strong.

But it is in the Book of Daniel that we have the most significant reflection of the state of mind into which patriotic Jews were thrown by the exciting events of this period. While the narratives in the book have a historical basis—the historicity of the prophet-statesman Daniel being unquestionable—it probably did not exist as we have it until the rising of the Maccabees. The author's thoughts manifestly revolve around Antiochus and the relations in which that monarch stood to the Jews; and, looking to the analogy of prophecy, it is difficult to accept the view that all these revelations respecting the Syrian king were vouchsafed to an exile in Babylon hundreds of years before the events took place. If, on the other hand, we regard the book as "the direct product of the Maccabean struggles,"[1] its point and significance are unmistakable. This hypothesis furnishes the key to its main design. Real prophecy was now a thing of the past; but the writer, as a Jewish patriot, desires to remind his fellow-countrymen that the God of Daniel is wont to observe and protect those who amid many trials continue in His fear, while at the same time He defeats the best laid schemes of the mightiest potentates. This is a strong consolation much needed by saints in those sore times, and his object is to nerve them to endure. The narratives of the first part of the book (I.-VI.) are all hortatory, and intended to encourage the victims of persecution to maintain the struggle, by placing before them some shining examples of piety from a former age. The prophetic visions of the future which make up the remainder of the book (VII.-XII.) go to show that the day of deliverance is at hand. As a nation,

---

[1] Schürer, who declares that "it is only as viewed in the light of this period that the book can be said to have either sense or meaning."—*The Jewish People in the Time of Jesus Christ*, div. ii. vol. iii. pp. 49, 52. For a detailed statement of the evidence, historical and linguistic, that can be adduced in favour of this date, see Driver's *Introduction to the Literature of the Old Testament*.

they have reached the thick darkness which precedes the dawn. The heathen dynasties are tottering to their fall ; the last and vilest of them is on the verge of being destroyed by the special intervention of the Almighty, who will, as soon as "the indignation is accomplished," transfer the dominion to Israel. Then "shall the saints of the Most High take the kingdom, and possess it for ever and ever" (vii. 18). This is the comforting truth which is fitted to sustain them even under the pressure of the dreadful ordeal to which meantime they are exposed.

BOOK IV

THE MACCABEAN PERIOD; OR, THE PERIOD OF FREEDOM, B.C. 167–135

———+———

CHAPTER I

THE JEWISH WAR OF INDEPENDENCE

1. The Hero of Modein.—While the Jews were drawing consolation from the Book of Daniel, there occurred an event which changed the whole aspect of affairs in Palestine. An aged priest, of the order of Joarib, Mattathias by name, and belonging to the family of the Asmoneans,[1] had withdrawn with his five sons from the persecution at Jerusalem to his native town of Modein, some twenty miles distant. In due course this quarter was visited by the king's myrmidons, with the view of extorting from every citizen a public acknowledgment of adherence to the Greek worship. Apelles, the chief commissioner, having summoned the inhabitants to offer sacrifice according to the pagan form, called upon Mattathias, as the foremost personage of the place, to lead the way. This he refused to do. When another Jew weaker

---

[1] From the circumstance of his tracing his descent to a man named Asamonaios, his family are known as "the Asmoneans." The names and surnames of his sons are Johannes Gaddi, Simon Thassi, Judas Maccabæus, Eleazar Avaran, and Jonathan Apphus. Little is known for certain regarding the origin and meaning of the various surnames. It is at least probable, however, that they were not intended to be symbolic, but were simply used for purposes of better designation.

than himself approached the heathen altar with an offering, the noble priest rushed forward and slew both him and the king's commissioner, and tore down the altar. The signal was thus given for open rebellion all over the land ; and in this unpremeditated way there arose in the providence of God a religious war, which was to end in the victorious restoration of the Jewish worship.

No longer safe in Modein, Mattathias invited all the faithful to follow him, and fled with his sons into the mountains.   Meanwhile many other fugitives from various quarters vainly sought concealment in the wilderness; being pursued by their persecutors, who studiously chose a Sabbath day for their attack, they tamely submitted to be slain rather than handle a weapon on that day. Mattathias and his followers determined to adopt a more spirited policy, and to meet force with force even upon the Sabbath. They were now joined by the Assideans, and by as many as were prepared to fight for their ancestral faith.   Mattathias thus found himself at the head of a band of insurgents, who commenced a sharp guerilla warfare against the Syrian oppressors.   They went up and down the country, overthrowing heathen altars, slaying apostates, enforcing circumcision, and reviving Jewish rites.   The death of Mattathias in B.C. 167–166, ere the work was well begun, came as a heavy blow to these zealous Israelites ; but happily for the future of the movement, the direction of it still remained in his family.   Five valiant sons were left to carry out his solemn charge to give their lives for the covenant of their fathers.

2. **Judas Maccabæus.**—In accordance with the recommendation of Mattathias, who had advised his sons to take Simon as their counsellor and Judas as their captain, the latter now assumed the conduct of the war.   He was the third son of Mattathias, and bore the surname Makkabaios,[1] from which his adherents

---

[1] The derivation of the name has been much contested.   The meaning now usually ascribed to it is that of the " Hammerer," although in a treatise on " The Name Machabee," Curtiss maintains that it signifies the " Extinguisher " (viz. of his enemies).

generally have received the name of Maccabees. A better leader could not have been found. Enemies flew terror-stricken before him ; friends entered at his call upon projects which in their cooler moments they would have pronounced impracticable. Like our own General Gordon, he combined in a remarkable way military genius with absolute faith in God. To such a man nothing was impossible. In his hands the struggle soon passed beyond the phase it had already assumed ; and henceforth we have to do, not with mere night skirmishes, but with regular war. In B.C. 166 the Syrian general Apollonius, who led an army out of Samaria against him, was defeated and slain ; and in the same year Seron, the governor of Cœle-Syria, was routed at Beth-horon. His fame was now secure : " all nations talked of the battles of Judas."

These disasters drove Antiochus nearly frantic, and only the impoverished condition of his treasury prevented him from swooping down upon Judea. Choosing to march against some eastern provinces which had been withholding tribute, he left his western domains as well as his youthful son Antiochus in charge of his kinsman Lysias, whom he also commissioned to destroy the Jewish nation root and branch, and to people the land with strangers. For this purpose he had left the half of his available troops, and Lysias lost no time in despatching a strong force against Judea under command of three trusted generals, Ptolemy, Nicanor, and Gorgias. The result was so far discounted that Syrian merchants were in the camp ready to buy up the Israelites as slaves ; but between them and the realisation of their hopes lay the generalship of Judas Maccabæus. While the Syrian army encamped at Emmaus, the faithful Israelites gathered at Mizpah. On this sacred height they observed a day of prayer and fasting in preparation for the impending battle. Before God they exhibited the affront put by the heathen upon their faith ; they spread out a copy of the Law painted over with heathen pictures ; they brought the priestly garments which could not be used, and the offerings which could not be presented ; they pointed to the Nazarites whose days were fulfilled, but whom they were powerless to release from their vows. After they had breathed a common prayer to Heaven, Judas set about organising his company into a regular army. He exempted from service all those for whose case the law had made provision,[1] so that no one might show himself listless or cowardly in battle. Straightway he left Mizpah, and pitched his camp on the south side of Emmaus. Adroitly turning to his own advantage a stratagem of the Syrian general's, who thought with a detachment of 6000 men to surprise the Jewish camp at night, Judas and his followers suddenly abandoned their position and moved on to attack the main body of the king's army, while Gorgias vainly wandered about seeking them among the mountains. With 3000 poorly armed men he confronted at break of day the Syrian host and put them to flight. Gorgias and his contingent returned only to see the smoke of their burning tents, and the Jews marshalled for battle, whereupon they also fled in confusion. Much booty fell into the hands of the victors, who went home praising the Lord in grateful songs.

Lysias now resolved to proceed against Judea in person ; and the next year, B.C. 165, saw an army of 60,000 foot and 5000 horse enter the country from the south by way of Idumea. But Judas with 10,000 men met them at Beth-zur on the road from Jerusalem to Hebron, and was again victorious. With 5000 dead upon the field, Lysias deemed it prudent to retire to Antioch and raise an army against which the little handful of Jews, valiant as they were, could not hope to stand.

3. **Re-dedication of the Altar.**—Judas availed himself of this temporary lull in the hostilities to re-establish the Jewish worship on Zion. Deep sorrow filled the hearts of the faithful when they beheld the neglected state of the sacred courts. Although the citadel still remained in the hands of a Syrian

---

[1] See Deut. xx. 5-8 ; 1 Macc. iii. 5, 6.

garrison, the vigilance of Judas kept them at bay until pious priests had cleansed the sanctuary. The polluted altar was pulled down; the sacred furniture was restored in accordance with the provisions of the law; and on the 25th Chisleu, B.C. 165, the very day on which three years before the heathen had first profaned it, the temple was reconsecrated by the offering of sacrifice on the newly-erected altar. The Feast of the Dedication was celebrated for eight days, and remained an annual observance while the temple stood. As soon as the festivities were over, Judas set about fortifying the temple mount. Defensive works were also undertaken at the important southern frontier town of Beth-zur, which was held by a Jewish garrison. With the purification and fortification of the temple, and the restoration of the ancient worship, the first stage in the history of the Jewish war of independence comes to a close. It is a record of unbroken victory, and a bright illustration of the power of a noble enthusiasm. Thanks to the valour of the Maccabees, Jewish religion was not only as yet not destroyed, but established more firmly than ever upon the basis laid down by Ezra the Scribe.

4. Jewish Military Aggression.— The success which had attended the Maccabees in war was distasteful to the heathen tribes around, and these now subjected all Jews in their vicinity to a relentless persecution. This caused Judas once more to take the field. Edomites, Beanites (otherwise not known), and Ammonites having been severally discomfited, he returned to Judea, but only to receive further pressing calls for relief from Gilead and Galilee. It was determined in both cases to send the help implored. Simon marched to Galilee with 3000, and Judas to Gilead with 8000 men. Both expeditions proved successful. Simon pursued his enemies as far as Ptolemais, and then escorted the rescued Jews to a place of safety in Judea. This policy of strengthening the Jewish power at the centre was also acted upon by Judas, who took the city of Bosra and the

various towns of Gilead, gathered together all the Israelites in
that region, and with them set out for Judea.   The fortified city of
Ephron, which refused them passage, was taken, and all its male
inhabitants put to the sword.   Returning to Judea, in B.C. 163,
without loss of a single man, they joyfully offered sacrifice upon
the holy mountain.   Meanwhile Joseph and Azariah, "captains of
the garrison," who had been left in charge at Jerusalem, were so
anxious to emulate the deeds of the Maccabees, that, despite the
caution given them by Judas, they made war against Gorgias in
Jamnia.   They were, however, miserably beaten, and lost 2000
men ere they regained the frontier.   From the standpoint of the
writer of 1 Maccabees, nothing else was to be expected, for
"these men came not of the seed of those by whose hand deliverance was given unto Israel."   The national hopes were
centred in "the man Judas and his brethren," who now made a
fresh raid upon the Edomites, and destroyed the old fortress of
Hebron.   But the closing scene in this chapter of Jewish
offensive warfare was enacted in the land of the Philistines.
Marching thither by way of the town of Mareshah, they
arrived in the region of Ashdod, pillaged the towns, pulled
down the altars of the heathen, and burned their idols.   These
iconoclastic measures showed that what had at first been
merely a movement in defence of Jewish religion, had already
assumed the form of a campaign to re-establish the Jewish
State.

5. Death of Antiochus Epiphanes, and Concession of Religious
Liberty.—The government of Syria had meanwhile undergone an
important change.   In B.C. 164, Antiochus Epiphanes, after a
reign of fourteen years, unexpectedly died.   Foiled in an attempt
to rob the rich temple of Nanea in Elymais, he fell back upon
Babylon, but only to hear of the defeat of his armies in Judea.
He appears to have taken these reverses much to heart.   Nor,
according to the Jewish historian, did he escape the tortures of
an accusing conscience with respect to the wrongs he had done

at Jerusalem; for to this cause he ascribed his troubles, and "perished through grief in a strange land."

Difficulties as to the succession materially influenced the further development of the struggle for religious freedom. Epiphanes had nominated Philip, one of his officers, as guardian to the minor Antiochus V. (Eupator); but Lysias, who had no notion of letting power slip out of his hands, arrogated this function to himself; while Demetrius, the rightful heir, who had been supplanted by Epiphanes, vainly sought to push his claims at Rome. Practically, therefore, the sovereignty remained with Lysias; but his zeal for the supremacy of Hellenism in Judea was as nothing to that of the despot who had died. Men of influence at the Syrian Court appear even to have wished to pacify the Jews by just and generous treatment (2 Macc. x. 12), and it seemed as if they might remain unmolested; but things fell out otherwise. Deeming the time opportune, Judas had laid siege to the fortress of Jerusalem, the sole outpost now held by the Syrian garrison. Certain of the besieged contrived to escape, and along with some Jewish apostates made a strong appeal to the king for help. Then at length, in view of these entreaties, and of the fact that Philip had gone to Egypt, and might induce Ptolemy Philometor to take up arms against Syria, it was determined to suppress the revolt in Judea. With an army of 100,000 infantry, 20,000 horsemen, and 32 trained elephants, Lysias and the young king besieged Beth-zur. Abandoning his attack on Acra, Judas made a gallant attempt to relieve the fortress, but in vain. At Beth-zachariah he suffered a serious defeat, and the loss of his younger brother Eleazar, who with magnificent indiscretion fought his way to the finely-caparisoned elephant on which the king was said to be riding, and stabbed the animal from beneath, but was himself killed by the falling carcase. The victorious Syrians marched straight upon Jerusalem, and besieged the temple mount. Unfortunately for the Jews, it happened to be the Sabbatic year, and the garrisons in both strongholds were ill-provided against a siege. Beth-zur was forced to capitulate, and Mount Zion was also on the point of yielding, when suddenly, owing to urgent affairs of state which rendered imperative his presence in Antioch, Lysias deemed it advisable to come to terms with the Jews. Philip was trying to force his way to the regency; and in order to have a free hand against him, Lysias at once ceded to the Jews by treaty all that they had been fighting for. They were to be as they had been prior to the reign of Epiphanes—politically subject, but religiously free. On this understanding they yielded the fortress; but the king still judged it best to demolish the strong wall by which it was surrounded. He then returned to Antioch, and soon took the city out of the hands of Philip.

With the concession of religious liberty, another important stage in the conflict is reached. Henceforth there was no attempt to Hellenise the Jews by force. They had successfully asserted the sacred rights of conscience, and preserved intact their own peculiar institutions and customs. This fact had necessarily the greatest significance for " the pious," who, though prepared to die rather than part with religious freedom, would not follow the Maccabees in fighting for political independence. The struggle was now to proceed upon an entirely different basis: it became essentially a contest for supremacy between the Greek party and the champions of the law.

CHAPTER II

FURTHER DEVELOPMENTS

1. **Party Strife between Judas Maccabæus and Alcimus, the newly-appointed Aaronic High Priest.**—On the advice of Lysias, Eupator gave up the hated Menelaus to an ignominious death; and Alcimus, who was at least of Aaron's line, was installed as high

priest. This promotion, however, he owed not to any special claims of his own, but to the fact that he was likely to prove a pliable tool in the hands of the government. Meanwhile, in B.C. 162, with the assistance of the historian Polybius, Demetrius I. (Soter) had escaped from Rome and landed at Tripolis. Advancing to Antioch, he took possession of the Syrian throne, and had both Lysias and his ward put to death. This change in the political situation brought to a point the opposition between the rival factions in Judea. Alcimus and his supporters approached the new king with complaints against Judas and his brethren, whom they represented as rebels against the monarchy and enemies to peace. Demetrius accordingly confirmed Alcimus in his office, and sent a large army under Bacchides into Judea to force the recognition of his nominee, and to seize the person of Judas. Now that they had "a priest of the seed of Aaron," the Assideans saw no reason for further opposition. But the confidence of Judas was not so easily won : he distrusted the fair promises which were being made. The soundness of his judgment was proved by the insane conduct of Alcimus, who, under cover of Bacchides and his troops, slew sixty of the Assideans in one day. The Syrian general, on returning to Antioch, left a contingent of troops to protect Alcimus. But Judas soon became too strong for them, and by his masterful treatment of apostates induced a reign of terror throughout the land. Alcimus was obliged once more to repair to the Syrian Court for assistance. Demetrius sent another army into Judea under Nicanor, who first of all made a mean but abortive attempt to seize Judas by stratagem. A battle followed at a place called Capharsalama, and ended in the defeat of Nicanor, who fell back upon Mount Zion. There he took occasion to insult the priests, and swore that unless Judas and his followers were delivered up to him, he would on his triumphant return burn up their temple. Proceeding to Beth-horon, he awaited the arrival of fresh troops from Syria. With only 3000 men Judas lay entrenched in Adasa. The battle was fought on the 13th Adar 161. Nicanor was himself the first to fall, and his army fled. For a whole day the troops of the Hammerer pursued them, and, with the help of the population in the different towns of Judea, hemmed them in and slew them to a man. The head and hand of the blasphemer were publicly "hung up toward Jerusalem"; and the 13th Adar, the day before the Feast of Purim, was afterwards kept as "Nicanor's day." This victory near the scene of one of his early triumphs won over to the side of Judas Maccabæus the entire Jewish nation. He was the popular hero once more.

2. **Last Days of Judas Maccabæus.** — Judas was resolved to abjure the Syrian yoke, and with this object made an appeal to the great power of Rome. Two Jewish ambassadors, Eupolemus and Jason, were favourably received by the Roman Senate, and a treaty concluded. Its provisions were graven on brass tablets and sent to Jerusalem; they were, however, rather vague, and nothing came of the agreement. A message was sent, indeed, to Demetrius, warning him that further molestation of the Jews would mean war with Rome; but the Syrian king had so far anticipated this interference that the power of Judea had been effectually crushed before it could take effect. In April 161, within two months after the defeat of Nicanor, Demetrius sent a fresh army to Judea under Bacchides. Judas had but 3000 men at Eleasa, and of these all but 800 deserted him when they saw the fearful odds against which they had to contend. Even those who remained faithful dissuaded him from entering on such a battle; but, with a true spirit of knight-errantry, Judas refused to retire. The battle lasted from morning till night. Judas and his best men broke the enemy's right wing, and were in full pursuit, but the left wing veered round and attacked them in the rear. A fierce conflict ensued; but when at last their brave leader fell, the Jewish survivors took to flight. The body of Judas was secured by his brothers, and interred amid a nation's tears in the family sepulchre at Modein.

Perhaps no leader of a forlorn hope ever succeeded to the extent that Judas did; yet the unequal contest in which he had engaged could have only one end. It was impossible for the Jewish people to hold their own in war against the imperial power of Syria; and the flourishing condition to which the Maccabean party afterwards attained, must be ascribed more to the factions that rent the Syrian Empire than to any inherent strength of its own.

3. **A Jewish Temple at Leontopolis.**—One result of the situation in Palestine appeared in a bold attempt to transfer the headquarters of Judaism to Egypt. In the reign of Ptolemy Philometor there fled into that country Onias IV., son of the high priest Onias III., who was murdered by Menelaus. Under the friendly shelter of the Egyptian Court, he conceived a plan whereby at once his own rights as legitimate high priest and the interests of Alexandrian Jews would be conserved. This was to establish a temple in Egypt itself. Having observed in the district of Heliopolis, near the city of Leontopolis, an old heathen sanctuary in ruins, he obtained leave from Ptolemy and his queen Cleopatra to set up there a temple similar to that at Jerusalem. A grant of crown lands was also made for its maintenance. This royal complaisance may have been partly due to the traditional alliance between the Ptolemies and the high-priestly house, but was mainly prompted by the desire to see the wealth of the Egyptian Jews kept in the country instead of being drained into Jerusalem. A regular staff of priests and Levites officiated at Leontopolis, which acquired considerable sanctity in the eyes of the Hellenists. Onias found scriptural authority for his action in the prophecy of Isa. xix. 18, 19, that there should one day be "an altar to Jehovah in the midst of the land of Egypt," and claimed that the very spot was marked out in the expression "city of the Sun."[1] This Egyptian temple declined in import-

[1] The place is rich in historical interest. It is mentioned under the names of On (Gen. xli. 45) and Beth-shemesh (Jer. xliii. 13). Joseph's father-in-

ance as soon as the Maccabean party fairly got the upper hand in Judea, and an Aaronic high priest ministered at the altar in Jerusalem. It still remained, however, a favourite resort of the Egyptian Jews until its destruction in the reign of Vespasian.

4. Jonathan chosen Successor to Judas.—To the Jewish nationalists the death of Judas proved a stunning blow. The Greek party, with Alcimus at their head, were again masters of the situation ; for Bacchides "chose the wicked men and made them lords of the country." But the Maccabees elected as their leader Jonathan, who, if inferior to his brother Judas as a soldier, surpassed him in diplomatic wisdom. Already the conflict had become political, and in the hands of Jonathan, who manifestly fought for his own house, it did so more and more. His party could not at first contemplate regular warfare ; they could only exist as freebooters.

The death of Alcimus in B.C. 160, following closely upon his sacrilegious interference with the inner court of the temple, was regarded as a divine judgment. No successor to the high priesthood appears to have been appointed by the Syrians, who were presumably tired of having always to protect this functionary by force of arms. Bacchides now returned to Antioch, and for two years Judea had rest. The effect of this was to strengthen greatly the Maccabean party. Their opponents invoked once more the aid of Bacchides, engaging to deliver Jonathan into his hands forthwith. The latter, however, got wit of the plot, and retaliated by slaying about fifty of those who had hatched it. Thereafter he entrenched himself in the wilderness at Beth-basi,

law was a priest of the Sun-worship practised in its famous temple, and under his learned successors Plato studied. The visitor to Heliopolis is shown an ancient sycamore, under which, according to tradition, Joseph and Mary rested when they fled with the child Jesus into Egypt. But the oldest monument of the locality is the spendid granite obelisk—the only one now remaining out of the many that once adorned the temple of the Sun—erected in the reign of Sesertesen I., founder of the 12th dynasty, *cir.* 2050 B.C. Heliopolis, which is situated about 8 miles to the north-east of Cairo, is now quite a small township.

and awaited the Syrian general, who besieged the fortress in vain. Jonathan made successful raids in the desert, and Simon severely punished the besiegers. Irritated by these reverses, Bacchides fell out with his advisers and put many of them to death. Jonathan proposed an armistice, and to this Bacchides, who was heartily sick of the whole business, agreed. He undertook never again to lift a finger against the Jewish nation.

From his residence at Michmash, Jonathan, no longer a party leader, but the hero who had won peace with honour for his nation, governed the people after the manner of the ancient Judges. The removal of Syrian coercion showed that the Greek party had no hold upon the hearts of the Jewish people. They were glad to renounce Hellenism for the law. Jonathan was now free to work at the problem of Jewish independence. He shrewdly availed himself of Syria's troubles, and was ever ready to trim his sail to the advantage of his nation. Rivals for the throne of the Seleucidæ now found it worth their while to compete for the favour of the Maccabees. When accordingly, in B.C. 152, Alexander Balas, ostensibly as the son of Antiochus Epiphanes, but in reality a tool in the hands of the king's enemies, seized Ptolemais and laid claim to the crown, Demetrius lost no time in making friendly overtures to Jonathan. He empowered him to raise an army and to liberate the hostages in Acra. Thereupon Jonathan took possession of Jerusalem, and began to fortify the city and the temple mount. The only places of refuge left for the Hellenisers were the citadel of Jerusalem and Beth-zur.

5. **Jonathan made High Priest.**—But Alexander Balas knew better how to prepare the bait for the ambitious Jonathan. He sent him a purple robe and a crown of gold, saying, "We ordain thee to be the high priest of the nation, and to be called the king's friend." Jonathan accepted this offer, donned the sacred robes at the Feast of Tabernacles, and gratefully espoused the cause of Balas. Demetrius now in turn tried to outbid his rival. But Jonathan declined to change sides: he distrusted Demetrius,

10

and he had faith in the ultimate ascendancy of Balas as the ally of Rome. The event proved the wisdom of his choice, for in the battle that ensued Demetrius I. was defeated and slain, and the victorious Balas heaped rewards upon Jonathan. At Ptolemais, where in B.C. 150 he married the Egyptian princess Cleopatra, he received the Jewish high priest with every mark of favour.

Jonathan soon had an opportunity of showing his fidelity towards the worthless Balas. In B.C. 147, Demetrius II. came from Crete to claim the throne. He secured an adherent in Apollonius, the governor of Cœle-Syria, but Jonathan declared against him. This led to hostilities between Apollonius and Jonathan, in which the former had the worst of it. His garrison at Joppa was forced to capitulate ; he lost a pitched battle at Ashdod ; and the temple of Dagon, in which his scattered horsemen had taken refuge, was burnt down. In consideration of these services, Alexander presented Jonathan with a buckle of gold, and with the city and lands of Ekron. But Balas had nearly reached the end of his career. His father-in-law, Ptolemy Philometor, having marched into Syria, Jonathan met him at Joppa and accompanied him to the river Eleutherus, but returned to Jerusalem on ascertaining that he had allied himself to Demetrius II. The high priest could not, however, save Alexander from disaster. After taking back Cleopatra and giving her to Demetrius as his wife, Ptolemy entered Antioch and assumed the crown of Asia. Alexander, defeated in battle, fled to Arabia, where he perished by the hand of an assassin. Ptolemy, who had been wounded in the fray, lived only to see brought to him the severed head of his former son-in-law. In B.C. 145, Demetrius became king.

Jonathan now laid siege to the tower of Jerusalem ; but, at the instance of "the ungodly," Demetrius summoned him to Ptolemais. With great *savoir faire* Jonathan took with him an imposing retinue of priests and elders, besides rich presents for the king, and secured not only his position as high priest, but almost all the concessions which he had refused to accept from Demetrius I. as the price of his adherence. The boundaries of Judea were enlarged, and 300 talents annually were to be paid in lieu of tribute.

6. The Treachery of Trypho. — Soon afterwards Demetrius caused great dissatisfaction by dismissing his regular troops. A certain Trypho took the opportunity to bring forward Antiochus, son of Alexander Balas, as a claimant for the crown. At the same time Jonathan boldly applied for the cession of the citadel of Jerusalem and other fortresses of Judea, and to this Demetrius consented, on condition that the Jews should come to his aid against the rebels of Antioch. The high priest sent 3000 men, who turned the scale in the king's favour. But Demetrius did not keep faith with his Jewish ally; Acra was still held by the Syrians. Jonathan accordingly went over to the side of Trypho, who had made himself master of Antioch, and who not only confirmed the high priest in all his honours, but also appointed his brother Simon commander for Palestine. Ostensibly in the interests of Syria, Jonathan now overran and subdued the whole territory between Jerusalem and Damascus. Ascalon opened its gates to him ; Gaza he captured, and forced to send hostages to Jerusalem. Leaving Simon to reduce Beth-zur, Jonathan met the generals of Demetrius on the plain of Hazor. A sudden onset by a party of Syrians, who had lain in ambush, caused his troops to flee ; but the sight of the high priest rending his robes revived their courage, and their loss was soon retrieved. After this, Jonathan, repeating the policy inaugurated by Judas, sent ambassadors to Rome and Sparta to establish friendly relations with these powers. Finding himself again menaced by the armies of Demetrius, he marched northwards to meet them at Hamath ; but on learning that their plan of a night-attack was discovered, the Syrians withdrew. The Jewish leader accordingly turned towards the desert of Arabia, and subdued the Zabadeans ; he also occupied Damascus. Meanwhile Simon garrisoned Joppa and fortified Adida, a town between Joppa and Jerusalem.

On his return to the capital Jonathan strengthened the fortifications and isolated the citadel.

Trypho now began to look askance upon the powerful ally who had enabled him to get the better of Demetrius. Secretly coveting the throne for himself, he feared that Jonathan might frustrate his designs. He therefore resolved to get rid of him. Cunning as he was, Jonathan let himself fall into a trap. Under pretext of gifting Ptolemais to him, Trypho induced him to accompany him to that city with only 1000 men. As soon as he had entered the gates he was made a prisoner, and his men were put to the sword.

7. **Leadership of Simon.**—At this juncture it was inevitable that Simon, the only one now left of the five brothers of the Maccabees, should come to the front. Immediately he pushed on the work of fortifying the city, and saw to the occupation of Joppa. Trypho soon invaded Judea, with Jonathan as his prisoner. Simon intercepted him at Adida. Trypho pretended that he held Jonathan in ward because he had not paid his imperial dues, and offered to release him on receiving 100 talents of silver and two of his sons as hostages. More trickery, thought Simon; yet, to silence criticism, he acquiesced. As he had expected, Jonathan was still kept a prisoner. Trypho then sought to reach Jerusalem by way of Adora on the south, but found himself checkmated by Simon at every point. The starving occupants of Acra appealed to him for supplies; but when his horsemen were ready to proceed, a fall of snow blocked the route through the wilderness. Foiled and irritated, he led his troops round the Dead Sea to Gilead, and at a place called Bascama took a mean revenge by putting Jonathan to death (B.C. 143). Simon recovered his body, and buried him in the family ground at Modein, over which he also erected a splendid tomb, which was visible from the Mediterranean. This was more than a family monument: it was an education to youth, an inspiration to posterity. While it stood, the sons of Israel would

be reminded of the heroic band of brothers whose prowess and patriotism had delivered their land from an alien yoke, and would, while thus constrained to honour the Maccabees, be also likely to imbibe something of their spirit.

8. Declaration of Jewish Independence.—It was given to Simon to put the copestone on the work which had been begun and developed by the other members of his house. Judas had fought and won the battle of religious freedom ; Jonathan had secured for his party the control of affairs in Judea ; and now under Simon the Jewish people actually regained their independence. In the contest between Demetrius and Trypho for the Syrian crown, Simon took no part further than to renew the friendship with Demetrius, who acknowledged him as high priest and king's friend, remitted all arrears of taxes, and granted exemption from tribute for the future. "Thus the yoke of the heathen was taken away from Israel." The political emancipation of the Jews was at last an accomplished fact, and they signalised it by adopting a new mode of reckoning. The Seleucid year 170, or B.C. 143, corresponded with the first year of Simon, the high priest, governor, and leader of the Jews. All Jewish documents were now dated according to this new era.

Although freedom had been conceded to Israel, Simon did not lie on his oars. He determined to capture the fortresses of Gazara and Jerusalem. The one was necessary to protect his frontier and cover the haven of Joppa ; so long as the other was held by the Syrians, Jewish freedom could be little more than a name. After some resistance Gazara capitulated. Simon cast out the heathen, "placed such men there as would keep the law," and appointed his son John ruler of the city. He also made himself master of Acra. That fortress was practically impregnable, but the garrison were at last starved into submission. In effectually separating the tower from the city, Jonathan had sowed, and now Simon reaped. All along it had been the ambition of the Maccabees to possess this stronghold ;

and after it had been duly purified, Simon entered it in triumph on the 23rd May, B.C. 142. He further asserted the independence of his rule by the issue of a new coinage in silver and copper,[1] and by renewing the treaties with Sparta and Rome.

9. Simon's Official Rank declared Hereditary.—The kings of Syria being no longer in a position to intermeddle in Judea, Simon set himself to promote the inner well-being of his country. As an administrator he surpassed all his brethren. Under his wise guidance trade and agriculture, law and social order, simultaneously began to flourish. It was a time of moral and material prosperity unequalled since the Exile. "Then did they till their ground in peace, and the earth gave her increase, and the trees of the field their fruit. The ancient men sat all in the streets, communing together of good things, and the young men put on glorious and warlike apparel. He provided victuals for the cities, and set in them all manner of munition, so that his honourable name was renowned unto the end of the world. He made peace in the land, and Israel rejoiced with great joy; for every man sat under his vine and his fig-tree, and there was none to fray them : neither was there any left in the land to fight against them : yea, the kings themselves were overthrown in those days. Moreover he strengthened all those of his people that were brought low : the law he searched out; and every contemner of the law and wicked person he took away. He beautified the sanctuary, and multiplied the vessels of the temple" (1 Macc. xiv. 8-15).

---

[1] The silver coins struck were of the value of a shekel and a half-shekel. Several specimens of them are still extant. They do not bear Simon's name, but are ascribed by most numismatists to his reign. The right of coinage was not formally granted to the Jews till about B.C. 140 (1 Macc. xv. 6); but it seems probable that the appearance of the new coins which bear the year numbers 1, 2, 3, 4, was coincident with the era of Simon alluded to in 1 Macc. xiii. 42. These Jewish coins were prepared from the Greek models, but with due regard to the precept against graven images. They are, however, tastefully executed, and adorned with figures of sacred cups, lily blossoms, palms, grape-clusters, etc. On one side they bear the inscription "Jerusalem the holy," and on the other "Israel's shekel" or "half-shekel."

It was fitting that such services to the nation should be publicly recognised. On the 18th September, B.C. 141, at a vast assembly of the priests, people, rulers and elders of the land, the offices of high priest, commander, and ethnarch were conferred upon Simon "for ever" (*i.e.* as hereditary possessions), "until there should arise a faithful prophet" (*i.e.* either the Messiah Himself, or His immediate forerunner ; or, more generally, until God should otherwise direct). Thus arose the new high-priestly dynasty of the Asmoneans.

10. Last Days of Simon.—But darker days were in store for Simon. He was once more drawn into the vortex of Syrian politics. Trypho had murdered his ward Antiochus VI., and had also got rid of Demetrius II., who was held as a prisoner by the Parthians. But in B.C. 139, Antiochus VII. Sidetes, younger brother of Demetrius II., secured a following, and defeated Trypho at Dora ; and although he had shortly before written to Simon, and sought by lavish promises, including the right of coinage, to win his friendship, he now changed his policy. During the siege of Dora, Simon sent him gifts and 2000 auxiliaries. This proffered help was declined, and a demand made for the surrender of Joppa, Gazara, and the fortress of Jerusalem, or failing this for 1000 talents. Simon offered 100 talents for Joppa and Gazara. Antiochus at once sent his general Cendebeus to make war against the Jews. Simon, now an old man, intrusted his sons Judas and John with the conduct of the campaign. Near Modein they completely routed the Syrians. Judas was wounded, but John pursued the enemy as far as Ashdod.

Simon was no more molested by Antiochus. Yet he was not to die a natural death. His own son-in-law, Ptolemy, the rich commander over the plain of Jericho, coveted the supreme power, and waited for an opportunity to destroy the ruling family. This came to him in February B.C. 135, when, with his sons Mattathias and Judas, Simon was engaged upon a magisterial visitation of the townships of Judea. At Jericho they were invited by Ptolemy to a banquet in the castle of Dok, and treacherously slain.

More than a generation had passed since Mattathias struck the first blow for freedom to worship God. These thirty years form the most glorious epoch in Jewish history. The old priest's bravery had borne fruit in the remarkable achievements of his sons. Almost from the beginning, however, the scope of the contest had been altered. The battle for religious liberty had ended with the concession of Lysias ; after that the war was a war for independence. This involved, unfortunately, a departure from the ideal of a holy commonwealth cherished by the leaders after the Exile. The alliance with Rome, the merciless treatment of opponents, the unsatisfactory relations with the Syrian monarchy—these were severally sources of disaster for the future.

It is impossible not to admire the character of Judas. His piety and unselfish devotion to his country were unquestionable. The aims and methods of Jonathan were by no means of such an exalted type. Clever, cunning, and unscrupulous, he even used the priest's office as a ladder to power. In some respects Simon was the greatest of them all. The elevation of his subjects was as dear to him as the honour and prosperity of his house. He was a good priest and a born statesman—"the David of his age."

BOOK V

THE ASMONEAN DYNASTY, B.C. 135-63

CHAPTER I

John Hyrcanus and the Pharisees

1. **John Hyrcanus.**—Ptolemy intended Simon's third son, John Hyrcanus, governor of Gazara, to share the fate of his relatives. But John, warned in time, slew his would-be assassins, and immediately occupied Jerusalem. He also assumed the high-priestly dignity. Thereafter he laid siege to the fortress of Dagon, whither Ptolemy had retired on finding the gates of the capital closed against him. Only one thing stood between the murderer and the doom he merited. John's mother had fallen into his hands, and he not only had her tortured before her son's eyes, but threatened to hurl her headlong from the walls unless the siege were raised. This dastardly policy enabled Ptolemy to hold out until the Sabbatic year called the Jewish army to rest from war. He then had his prisoners slain, and fled across the Jordan.

In B.C. 135, Antiochus VII. Sidetes took the field in person against Hyrcanus. Having devastated Judea, he laid active siege to Jerusalem. The strength of the walls afforded no protection against famine ; and despite the valour of the besieged, who harassed the enemy by frequent sorties, the city was, after well-nigh a year, reduced to such straits that John drove out all

who were unfit for war.   But the Syrians would not allow them
to pass, and many perished of hunger before the survivors were
readmitted at the Feast of Tabernacles.   In order to observe
this festival, Hyrcanus applied for a seven days' truce, and
Antiochus wisely granted it.   Not only so, he even presented
splendid sacrificial gifts.   Thereupon the Jews designated him
Antiochus *the Pious*, and negotiated for peace.   He demanded
that they should deliver up their arms, pay tribute for Joppa and
other outlying possessions, and admit a Syrian garrison into
Jerusalem.   Instead of the last-named obnoxious condition,
Hyrcanus induced Antiochus to accept hostages and 500 talents
of silver.   After destroying the walls of Jerusalem, he withdrew
his army from Judea and fought against the Parthians.   In this
war Hyrcanus was associated with him as his vassal.   Judea had
thus already lost its hard-won independence ; the Syrian yoke
was once more a reality.

But in B.C. 128, Antiochus fell in the Parthian campaign, and
Demetrius II. was once more king of Syria.   A contest arose
about the succession, which enabled Hyrcanus to retrieve his
losses.   He extended the Jewish territory to its ancient dimensions.   In one respect his policy was certainly more worldly than
that of his predecessors.   With treasure abstracted from the
sepulchre of David he maintained a large body of foreign troops.
Thus reinforced, he took Medeba and other fortified cities east of
the Jordan.   Then, turning northwards, he captured Shechem,
and destroyed the Samaritan temple on Gerizim.   Finally,
marching to the south, he subdued Adora and Marissa, and gave
the Idumeans the alternative of accepting the Jewish law or
quitting the country.   They submitted to the rite of circumcision,
and so became merged in the Jewish nation.   Forced conver-
sions, however, are never satisfactory, and these Edomites proved
a disturbing element in the sacred community.

Continuing the policy of his predecessors, Hyrcanus now sought
to renew the alliance with Rome.   His immediate object was to
repudiate with some show of justice the bargain which he had

struck with Sidetes. The Jewish embassy was politely received, and as politely bowed out, by the Senate. In the times of the Gracchi the internal commotions of the Roman commonwealth were too serious to permit of interference in Syrian politics. After the death of Antiochus Sidetes, Syria became a prey to internal discord. At the instance of Ptolemy VII. Physcon, king of Egypt, Demetrius II. was displaced by a certain Alexander Zabinas (125), who in his turn was overthrown by Antiochus VIII. Grypos (122). The latter, after a reign of eight years, during which the Jews remained unmolested, was ousted by his step-brother Antiochus IX. Cyzicenus. To none of these kings did Hyrcanus pay tribute. " Neither as their subject nor as their friend did he any longer pay them the least regard," [1] but wisely occupied himself in furthering the interests of his country.

The closing event of John's reign was an expedition against the Samaritans, who in league with the Syrians had attacked the Jewish colony of Marissa. Having surrounded the city of Samaria with a trench and a double wall, he left his sons Antigonus and Aristobulus to conduct the siege. Twice over the Samaritans invoked the aid of Cyzicenus, but in neither case did it prove effectual. After holding out bravely for a year, Samaria was captured and razed to the ground. The Jewish legends tell that a heavenly voice announced to Hyrcanus the final victory of his sons while he was officiating in the temple. This was an experience like that of the banished Ezekiel when Jerusalem was taken by Nebuchadnezzar, and won for Hyrcanus the title of prophet. A special halo of sanctity was thus thrown round his high priesthood. Externally his reign (B.C. 135-105) was prosperous and even brilliant. He was the first Jewish prince whose name was stamped on the coins. Josephus eulogistically points out that God esteemed him worthy to fill the three offices of ruler, priest, and prophet. His was a bright image truly, and destined to become still more bright amid the thickening darkness of the days that were at hand.

[1] Josephus.

2. Rival Schools and Parties in Judea.—Closely connected with the Maccabean struggle, though not directly resulting from it, was the rise of political and religious parties in Israel. These really existed in germ before, but the conflicts of the period gave a strong impulse to their development and consolidation. The party of the Pharisees sprang from the scribes ; that of the Sadducees, from the priests. But the essential distinction between them was not, originally at least, a religious one ; it was rather practical and political. The Pharisees were above all the party of the law ; the Sadducees, that of the aristocracy.

(1) *The Pharisees.*—The new zeal with which the law was observed, and the diligent manner in which it was added to, soon opened the way for Pharisaism. The *Parûsh* was an exclusive separatist, not merely from the uncleanness of the heathen (Ezra vi. 21), but also from what he considered the uncleanness of multitudes of Jews. The term separatists, scornfully applied to them by their opponents, the Pharisees accepted as a title of honour. It was their aim to exemplify in practical life the punctilious legalism worked out by the scribes. Believing that nothing could hold the nation together but acts of piety, they attempted to create a principle of unity out of mere external uniformity of practice and profession. Under this system, as we see from the New Testament, piety became a trade, and men little better than religious machines. There were doubtless among the Pharisees a number of sincere and righteous men (John iii. 1), but as a class their righteousness was of a purely mechanical type (Matt. v. 20). They made ostentatious and long prayers, went about with advertisements of their piety pinned on to their clothes, and boasted before God and men of their good works and almsdeeds. These characteristics brought down upon them the severe denunciation of Jesus.

According to the Pharisees, the traditional or "oral" law was equally binding with the written law, and to teach in opposition to the former was even more criminal than to contradict the latter. Doctrinally, they were exponents of the orthodox form of later Judaism. They held the free activity and moral responsibility of man in conjunction with a full recognition of God's omnipotence and providence in all that comes to pass ; they maintained the existence of angels and spirits ; they believed in the immortality of the soul, in the resurrection of the body, and in future rewards and punishments.

It must be said for the Pharisees that they had the courage of their convictions. They endeavoured to live out their creed. In their view it was *the* business of the nation to keep the law, seeing that along this path alone could they inherit the promises. They therefore kept themselves studiously free from political entanglements, except in so far as they were obliged to contend for freedom to carry out the provisions of the law. So long as this was granted them, the particular government under which they lived was to them a matter of indifference. Their one concern was to secure Israel's fidelity to what they conceived to be her great mission, viz. to hasten on, by faithfulness to the covenant, the coming of the promised Deliverer. The Pharisees certainly rendered a great service in thus keeping alive the hope of a personal Messiah in an age when there was little living faith in this fundamental doctrine. Bound up with this also was their strenuous advocacy of the doctrine of the resurrection. Their teaching helped towards a much clearer apprehension of a future life than had obtained previously. Everlasting torment, they asserted, was laid up for the wicked ; but when the Messiah's kingdom should be established, the righteous would rise to share in its blessedness.

The Pharisees were the Assideans of a somewhat later date. They had no political ambitions, and fought along with the Maccabees only so long as the contest was one for religious freedom. Their influence, however, was paramount in Israel. This was due not so much, perhaps, to their democratic standpoint, as to the strictness of their religious practice. In these scrupulously holy ones the rank and file of the nation beheld their natural guides, and reverenced them as much as they were despised by them. The Pharisees did not shrink from the logical conclusion of their principles, and regarded the true Israel as confined to their own ranks.

(2) *The Sadducees.*—It can hardly be wondered at that an opposition party should have arisen in Israel, and that they carried their opposition to a very extreme point. These were the Sadducees, who probably derived their name from Zadok, the high priest in whose family the priestly office remained from the time of Solomon to the death of Onias III. As a party they were more select than numerous, and may be described as consisting of the priestly aristocrats and their adherents. Their spirit was as secular as that of the Pharisees was religious. As to their peculiar tenets, they refused to acknowledge the binding force of Pharisaic tradition ; they denied the existence of angels and spirits ; they rejected the belief in a resurrection of the body, in a final judgment, and in the immortality of the soul ; they held that man is the exclusive architect of his own fortunes, and that God takes nothing to do with human actions. This creed of theirs, which simply amounted to the negation of the Pharisaic position, was not so much the result of a conservative clinging to the older Hebrew standpoint, as of sheer and unadulterated worldliness. In matters religious they were disposed to be content with little. While maintaining a lofty contempt for questions of dogmatic theology, they showed a very keen front when it was proposed to interfere with any of their legal rights. It was the secular side of politics that they cared for. They valued the favour of a reigning prince far more highly than the observances of Mosaism. Although they professed to believe in the authority of the written law, they made the civil regulations of the State the measure of their obligations. Quite satisfied with common justice, they had no desire to be so excessively virtuous as the Pharisees, whose minute scrupulousness they held up to ridicule. "These Pharisees," they said, "will purify in the end the sun itself." In spite of the low tone of morality which the Greek supremacy had brought with it, they were anxious to engraft Greek freedom and

culture upon the national life and character. The antagonism between them and the Pharisees was thus really a secondary version of the old feud between the Hellenists and the Assideans. The spirit of the party, as subsequently developed, has been well caught and expressed in a sentence by *Thackeray* : " The Baptist might be in the wilderness, shouting to the poor who were listening with all their might and faith to the preacher's awful accents and denunciations of wrath, or woe, or salvation ; and our friend the Sadducee would turn his sleek mule with a shrug and a smile from the crowd, and go home to the shade of his terrace, and muse over preacher and audience, and turn to his roll of Plato, or his pleasant Greek song-book, babbling of honey and Hybla, and nymphs and fountains of love." As time went on the struggle between Sadducees and Pharisees became keener and keener. There could be only one issue to it. It was a conflict of Patricians with Plebeians, and the latter were constantly increasing in numbers and in power.

(3) *The Essenes.*—Writing for Greeks and Romans, Josephus speaks grandly of " three philosophical sects among the Jews " —the Pharisees, who corresponded to the Stoics ; the Sadducees, who were presumably the counterpart to the Epicureans ; and the Essenes, whose position he describes as akin to that of the Pythagoreans. This somewhat oblique presentation of the actual facts of the case has made it usual to reckon the Essenes as a third party in the Israelitish life of the period. But in truth these men represented not a political party, but a religious tendency. Their principles precluded them from interfering in public affairs. To all intents and purposes they were a monastic order, sworn to a life of asceticism and to secrecy respecting their peculiar doctrines. Their name and their origin are alike obscure.[1] In the time of Philo they numbered 4000, and lived chiefly in villages by themselves. Their favourite haunts were in the

---

[1] The most probable derivation of the name is from a Syriac word meaning *pious* ; and the first historical reference to them points to the middle of the second century B.C.

vicinity of the Dead Sea. The Essenes formed a communistic brotherhood, admission to which was signalised by the symbolic gifts of an axe, an apron, and a white robe, and completed only after a lengthened probation. Like the primitive Christians, they had all things common, and knew no distinction of purse, property, or house. Most of them were engaged in agriculture. They wore a special garb, forbade marriage, and abjured slavery and war, and even trade as conducive to covetousness.[1] While sending gifts to the temple, they did not offer sacrifices, "having more pure lustrations of their own."[2] In their excessive zeal for rigorous legalism and ceremonial purity, they surpassed the Pharisees as much as the Pharisees surpassed the general body of the people. The more effectually to separate themselves from everything unclean, they retired from public life altogether. Their common meals, prepared by one of their own priests, were as nearly as possible religious services ; "they go into the dining-room as into a certain holy temple." As a class the Essenes lived a life of great piety, simplicity, and gentleness. In their quiet retirement they showed much diligence in the study of Scripture ; and on this account, as well as by reason of their elaborate purifications, they came to be in high repute as foretellers of future events. In spite of their rejection of animal sacrifices, and their strange habit of turning in prayer, not towards the temple, but towards the sun, the general standpoint of the Essenes was essentially Jewish. No doubt these two peculiarities, together with some others, amount to a direct deviation from Judaism, and must be attributed to foreign influences of some sort. What these influences were—whether Syrian, Parsee, or Greek—can scarcely be determined. All that can be said with certainty is, that while Essenism had a truly Jewish basis, its straining after absolute purity led to results irreconcilable with genuine Judaism. As regards its non-Jewish

---

[1] Reuss describes Essenism as "a singular combination of estimable virtues, extravagant prejudices, and puerile forms."—*Apostolic Age*, i. p. 106.

[2] Joseph. *Ant.* xviii. 1. 5.

features, we may perhaps with Josephus ascribe them to the influence of the Pythagoreans.

3. Hyrcanus deserts the Pharisees.—The Maccabean party had been essentially Pharisaic in its origin, and John Hyrcanus was himself a valued disciple of the Pharisees. But the relative importance attached by them to political supremacy and religious praxis was gradually bringing about an estrangement between this powerful sect and the reigning high priest. The Pharisees cared nothing for political prestige ; all they wanted was freedom to carry out the provisions of the law. Hyrcanus, on the other hand, subordinated his zeal for the law to the worldly interests of his own house. An open rupture seems to have come about in a somewhat trivial manner. Josephus relates that on one occasion, when a number of Pharisees were his guests, Hyrcanus asked them to point out anything faulty in his conduct, that he might correct it. A certain Eleazar boldly said : " Since thou desirest to know the truth, if thou wilt be righteous in earnest, lay down the high priesthood and content thyself with the civil government of the people." Hyrcanus inquired the reason of this demand. As given by Eleazar, it was even more distasteful than the demand itself. "We have heard it from old men," said he, "that thy mother had been a captive under the reign of Antiochus Epiphanes." This, however, was false ; and Hyrcanus, greatly enraged, asked the Pharisees how such a slanderer should be dealt with. They adjudged him worthy of "stripes and bonds "; but with this mild verdict Hyrcanus was not satisfied. He suspected that Eleazar had expressed the real sentiment of his party, and that the Pharisees were anxious to strip him of his priestly dignity. He accordingly abandoned the sect, repudiated their traditions and their interpretation of the law, enacted penalties against the observance of their precepts, and formally joined the Sadducees. In the freer atmosphere breathed by the sons of Zadok the law need never clash with what he conceived to be conducive to the independence of the Jewish State. Hyrcanus was right in so far as his action was a moral protest against the Pharisaic mode of handling the law ; he was wrong in so far as it was a claim that the royal and the priestly power should be exercised by the same person. That the Pharisees entertained no imaginary distrust on this score, but perceived a real danger to all that they held sacred, events were soon to prove. The interests of religion were only too frequently sacrificed to the exigencies of worldly politics. In the history of the Asmonean princes we are already face to face with the problem of Church and State.

CHAPTER II

REVIVAL OF HELLENISM

1. Judas Aristobulus.—From the days of Hyrcanus, who was strong enough to weather even the opposition of the Pharisees, the Asmonean dynasty rapidly degenerated. John bequeathed the civil power to his wife, and the high priesthood to Judas Aristobulus, the eldest of his five sons. But Aristobulus resentfully imprisoned all his relatives except his brother Antigonus, and assumed the title of king, which no Jew had borne since the Exile. The coins, indeed, were inscribed with the simple name "Judas the high priest," for there were many in Israel who would own no earthly king, or at all events none outside the Davidic line. But the Greek proclivities of the young prince were very decided, and even won for him the surname of Phil-Hellen. The withdrawal of Hyrcanus from the Pharisees had initiated a reaction in favour of the Greek culture. He called his sons by Greek names, and they gave themselves up to Greek manners. In Aristobulus the civic ruler completely overshadowed the high priest. The work of the early Maccabees was already being undone by their own descendants. Not that every shred of genuine Jewish feeling had as yet departed from the Asmoneans. Aristobulus overran and annexed Iturea in the north of Palestine, and forced circumcision upon the inhabitants, as Hyrcanus had done in the case of the Idumeans in the south. After a brief reign of one year, which saw no other enterprise of consequence, he died of a painful disease. During his illness he was led to suspect that Antigonus meant to supplant him. He ordered his brother to come to him unarmed, and instructed his guards to slay him if he carried weapons. The very parties who aroused the king's suspicion now represented to Antigonus that Aristobulus desired him to present himself in new armour. The plot succeeded, and the innocent Antigonus was slain. Remorse for this crime is said to have precipitated the king's death. Strabo, quoted by Josephus, describes Aristobulus as "a man of candour, and very serviceable to the Jews." Possibly the accounts we have of his unnatural treatment of his relatives are coloured by the malice of the Pharisees.

2. **Alexander Jannäus: his Earlier Campaigns.** — Aristobulus left no son to succeed him. After his death, his widow, Salome Alexandra, liberated his three brothers, and made the eldest of them, Alexander Jannäus (Heb. Jannai=Jonathan), king and high priest. In accordance with Hebrew custom, she also became his wife. Alexander began his reign of twenty-six years (B.C. 104-78) by putting to death one of his brothers who aimed at the kingdom. He gave the same support to Hellenism as did his predecessor, and had his coins inscribed in Greek as well as in Hebrew. Essentially a man of war, Jannäus first of all set his heart on acquiring the coast of Philistia, and laid siege to Ptolemais. This brought him into collision with Ptolemy Lathurus, who had been expelled from Egypt by his mother Cleopatra, and had established himself in Cyprus. First the inhabitants of Ptolemais, and afterwards the people of Gaza,

invoked the assistance of this prince against Alexander. Aided
by the skilful generalship of Philostephanus, Ptolemy inflicted a
crushing defeat upon the Jews near the Jordan, and perpetrated
barbarous cruelties in the surrounding villages. This success
led Cleopatra to despatch a fleet and an army against him.
The Egyptian queen soon made herself mistress of Palestine,
and was advised to annex it. But her Jewish general Ananias
so resolutely opposed this course, that she consented to ratify
by treaty the independence of the Jewish State. Ptolemy then
judged it prudent to return to Cyprus. Alexander found a fresh
field for his warlike energies in the north-east of Palestine. He
took Gadara after a ten months' siege, and also the fortress of
Amathus. On the Philistine seaboard he captured Raphia and
Anthedon, and laid siege to Gaza. For a whole year this
ancient stronghold stood out, and ultimately fell into his hands
only through the treachery of Lysimachus against his brother
Apollodotus. How thoroughly Gaza had been Hellenised
appears from these names, and also from the fact that 500
senators were in *sederunt* at the time of the attack. Jannäus
gave over the city to fire and sword.

3. **Civil War between Jannäus and the Pharisees.**—But Jannäus
had to pay dearly for his victory. His dominions had been
extended at the cost of internal strife. The sons of Hyrcanus
identified themselves with the Sadducees ; but the party of the
law had nevertheless been steadily gaining in power and influence
with the people. It was no longer as in the days of the earlier
Asmoneans, when the popular enthusiasm made it impossible for
them to do more than take their own course as men who had to do
with God and the law, and not with war and politics. Thousands
of Jews were scandalised to see a man like Jannäus, whose hands
literally reeked with blood, discharging the functions of the
high priest. The ranks of the Pharisees were largely recruited
from those who were thus minded. On the king's return from
Gaza the smouldering discontent at last broke out. During the

Feast of Tabernacles he was pelted by the mob with the citrons which they were required to carry along with the festal palm-branch. They also reviled him as the son of a prisoner of war, and not worthy to fill the priest's office. Jannäus avenged this insult by ordering his foreign troops to fall upon the assembled multitude, of whom no fewer than 6000 were slain. After this exciting episode Alexander invaded Perea, and made tributary the Arab tribes who dwelt there. He also demolished Amathus. But his next movement was attended with disaster. During a battle with Obodas, king of Arabia, at Gadara in Gilead, he was caught in an ambush, lost all his troops, and barely escaped with his life to Jerusalem. The people then openly rebelled. For six years there raged a fierce civil war between the two opposing parties. The Sadducees sided with the king ; the Pharisees, with the populace at their back, tried to throw off his yoke. Mercenaries were hired on both sides, and 50,000 Jews are said to have lost their lives in the struggle. Wearied with the protracted misery, Jannäus besought the Pharisees to look on him with a kindlier eye ; but their bitterness knew no bounds. When he asked them what he could do to satisfy them, they told him to kill himself, and presently summoned to their aid Demetrius Eucärus, then governor of Damascus. Near Shechem a battle was fought ; Alexander was worsted, and fled to the mountains. A strange thing then happened to turn the scale once more in his favour. Out of pity for the helpless condition of the heir of the Maccabees, 6000 Jews from the opposite camp went over to Alexander. This reawakening of the national sentiment caused Demetrius to leave the country, and enabled Jannäus to suppress the revolt. He took a wolfish revenge on his Pharisaic foes. During a dissolute revel he had about eight hundred prisoners crucified, and while they were yet alive ordered their wives and children to be butchered before their eyes. After this his enemies, to the number of 8000, fled away in the night, and remained in exile as long as he lived. " Son of a Thracian " was the contemptuous epithet currently applied to him ; but so far as

the Pharisees were concerned he reigned henceforth in peace
The tranquillity of the land was, indeed, soon again to be dis-
turbed, but this time from without.

4. Later Campaigns of Alexander Jannäus—A contest for the
throne of the now tottering Syrian Empire was taking place
between Philip and Dionysius, the only surviving sons of
Antiochus Grypos. Dionysius was also conducting a campaign
against Aretas, king of the Arabians, and determined to proceed by way of Joppa to the trans-Jordanic region in order to
meet his enemy. Although Jannäus vainly endeavoured to
obstruct his passage through Judea, Antiochus fell in the battle
that ensued. Thereupon Aretas took possession of Cœle-Syria,
and defeated Jannäus at Adida. By mutual agreement, however,
the conqueror withdrew from Judea. Whatever were the terms
of the treaty with Aretas, the next three years (B.C. 84–81) were
devoted by Alexander to the reconquest of those districts east
of the Jordan which he had been forced to part with during
the civil war. Having captured Pella, Dium, and the wealthy
Gerasa, he marched northwards upon Golan and Seleucia, both
of which fell into his hands, as did also the fortress of Gamala.
Pella he laid waste because its inhabitants refused to embrace
Judaism. His dominions now equalled those of the ancient
Davidic kingdom—a result attained, however, at great cost of
men and means. Although physically enfeebled by his exertions
and excesses, Alexander Jannäus could not, during the three
years that yet remained to him, altogether rest from war. His
death, which was hastened by hard drinking, took place at the
siege of Ragaba in Perea, in B.C. 78.

CHAPTER III

PHARISAIC REACTION UNDER ALEXANDRA

1. **Alexandra (B.C. 78-69).**—The accession of Alexander's widow was signalised by a reversal of the policy pursued since the time of Hyrcanus. To the leading representatives of the Pharisees she declared her intention of conducting the affairs of the kingdom in accordance with their principles. The elated Pharisees gave a splendid funeral to their deceased antagonist, and even praised his virtues. Alexandra's elder son, Hyrcanus II., a spiritless weakling, was appointed high priest, while Aristobulus, the younger and more energetic, was studiously left out in the cold. All the Pharisaic observances abrogated by Hyrcanus were restored, and everything arranged to the liking of the new masters. While, however, she allowed them a free hand in moulding the internal life of the nation, the queen asserted her authority in the control of external affairs. By maintaining a strong army of foreign mercenaries, who might transgress the law without complaint from the Pharisees, she effectually secured the peace of the country.

The excessive zeal of the Pharisees, however, again threw the nation into a ferment. Instead of letting well alone, they urged the queen to punish by death those who had advised the crucifixion of the 800 rebels. But after Diogenes and other friends of Jannäus had been cut down, the leaders of the Sadducees openly remonstrated with Alexandra, and invoked her protection. To their representations were added the bitter reproaches of her own son, Aristobulus ; and the unhappy queen, utterly at a loss how to create a *rapport* between the two parties, handed over to the Sadducees all the fortresses except those of Hyrcania, Alexandrium, and Machærus. They now waited for a favourable opportunity to revolt. This came soon. As his mother lay

dangerously ill, the wily Aristobulus stole away from Jerusalem
by night, and within a fortnight got twenty-two fortresses to
declare for him. A large army flocked to his standard. The
news of these proceedings was carried to Alexandra's deathbed
by Hyrcanus and the elders, who besought her to intimate her
wishes. She reminded them that they had a nation in good
heart, an army, and a well-filled treasury ; these resources they
must use as they thought fit ; she was no longer for this world.
Alexandra then died (B.C. 69), in the seventy-third year of her
age and the ninth of her reign. In ambition she resembled
Athaliah, the only other woman who ever held the Jewish sceptre.

2. **Aristobulus II. (B.C. 69-63).**—The downfall of the Asmonean
house was now at hand. On the death of Alexandra, Hyrcanus
II., the high priest, assumed the government, but within three
months was compelled to retire in favour of his younger brother,
Aristobulus II. After his defeat in a battle at Jericho, many of
the soldiers of Hyrcanus went over to the opposite camp. He
then fled to the citadel of Jerusalem, and sued for peace. Fortunately for him, the wife and family of Aristobulus, who had
been shut up in the tower by Alexandra, still remained there ;
otherwise the conqueror might not have been so easy to deal
with. As it was, Aristobulus was willing that Hyrcanus should
live in Jerusalem and retain his private revenues, provided he
gave up all claim to the throne and the priesthood. To this
Hyrcanus agreed, and the two brothers publicly pledged themselves to observe the terms of the compact. The accession of
Aristobulus meant the disappearance of the Pharisaic influence
from the national councils, and the revival of the policy in vogue
prior to the reign of Alexandra. The law and its devotees were
alike thrust into the background. To another class also this
change of régime was distasteful. The foreign generals to whom
Alexandra had given the charge of her army must have perceived
that their position was no longer secure now that the Sadducees
were once more in power.

3. The Idumean Antipater.—But no one was more dissatisfied with the abdication of Hyrcanus than a certain Idumean called Antipater, who, together with his son Herod, was practically to shape the course of Jewish politics down to the Christian era. This man's father had been appointed governor of Idumea by Alexander Jannäus, and had sedulously ingratiated himself with the neighbouring tribes. The youthful Antipater pursued the same policy, and continued through life to act on the principle of self-aggrandisement by alliance with the powerful. As one having his own axe to grind, he had hoped much from his friendship with Hyrcanus, and looked with anything but equanimity on the elevation of his energetic opponent, Aristobulus. He accordingly resolved to secure, if possible, the restoration of Hyrcanus. First of all, he represented to prominent Jews the injustice of the arrangement whereby the younger son usurped the rights of the elder. Then he tried to persuade Hyrcanus that his life was in danger while his brother remained king. At first Hyrcanus would not listen, but after a while he was induced to flee to Petra, the capital of Aretas, who had agreed to give him a friendly reception. The scheming Idumean further got the Arabian monarch to promise to reinstate Hyrcanus in his kingdom, on condition that the latter should restore to him the twelve cities which Jannäus had taken from the Arabians. Aretas then marched against Aristobulus, and defeated him. This caused many of his troops to desert him for Hyrcanus, to whom the Pharisees and the bulk of the people also attached themselves. With a small following of priests, Aristobulus retired to the temple mount, where he was besieged by the Arabs and Pharisees. The *morale* of this coalition army seems to have been of the lowest type. According to Josephus, they got hold of a certain holy man called Onias, and desired him to invoke the curse of God on Aristobulus and his partisans. Onias entreated God to hearken to the prayers of neither party against their brethren, whereupon the bystanders, not appreciating such neutrality, stoned him to death. The besiegers also meanly withheld from the priests certain animals for sacrifice at the Feast of the Passover, although they had been paid for at the rate of a thousand drachmas each.

CHAPTER IV

CONQUEST OF PALESTINE BY THE ROMANS

1. The Arbitrament of Rome.—Meanwhile a new element entered into the situation. That intimate relationship with Rome which the Jewish leaders had once and again vainly sought to establish, they were now to experience, though scarcely in the form that they had anticipated. While Aristobulus was being besieged in Jerusalem, Pompey the Great was busied with his conquests in Asia. In B.C. 65, during the war with Tigranes, king of Armenia, he sent Scaurus into Syria. At Damascus that general heard enough to induce him to proceed forthwith to Judea, where both parties solicited his support. Scaurus decided in favour of Aristobulus, and ordered Aretas to withdraw, unless he chose to incur the enmity of the Romans. The restoration of Hyrcanus would have meant the supremacy of the Arabs in Palestine; and it was the policy of Rome to maintain the independence of the several petty kingdoms in Syria until they could be merged one by one in the great republic. Thus threatened, Aretas took himself off, and Scaurus returned to Damascus. Aristobulus, however, fell upon the retreating Arabians, and defeated them with great slaughter.

The appeal to the arbitrament of Rome was renewed in B.C. 64, on the arrival of Pompey himself at Damascus. Three separate parties appeared to state their case before him. Antipater claimed the crown for Hyrcanus as the legal heir, and denounced Aristobulus as a freebooter and a pirate; Aristobulus was represented by a certain Nicodemus, who urged the incapacity of Hyrcanus;

the Jewish people also, wearied with the degeneracy of the ruling house, sent an embassy, praying that the monarchy should be abolished, and that the ancient constitution, according to which the nation was subject only to the priests of God, should be restored. Although Aristobulus had prefaced his claim by sending a rich present to Pompey, the latter put off a final decision on the controversy. He had first, he said, to deal with the Nabateans; but afterwards he would visit Jerusalem in person, and settle their affairs. Dissatisfied with this temporising policy, Aristobulus marched by way of Dium across the Jordan, and entrenched himself in the mountain fortress of Alexandrium. Pompey deferred his expedition against the Nabateans, and advanced by Pella and Scythopolis to Coreae, against Aristobulus. The latter, after some parley, surrendered his fortresses, but fell back upon the capital, and prepared for war. Pompey, however, pitched his camp at Jericho, and in the morning appeared before the walls of Jerusalem. Aristobulus approached him with promises of money, and offered to surrender the city. But when Pompey despatched his favourite Gabinius to see that these conditions were fulfilled, the king's soldiers closed the gates against him. Aristobulus was thereupon thrown into prison, and Pompey in wrath attacked the city.

2. **Jerusalem besieged and occupied by the Romans.** — Inside the walls Jerusalem was divided against itself. Eventually the party of Hyrcanus got the upper hand, and surrendered the city. But the followers of Aristobulus withdrew to the temple mount, cut off the bridge, declined all terms, and prepared for a siege. Any assault on the temple was feasible from the north side only, and even there the fortifications were exceedingly strong. With much difficulty the Romans contrived to fill up the deep moat, and to place their battering-rams in position. It was only by utilising the Sabbaths, when the Jews would not handle a weapon, save in self-defence, that these measures were accomplished. After a three months' siege, a breach was made in the fortifica-

tions.   A son of the dictator Sulla was the first to scale the wall.
The Romans poured in at his heels, and the sacred precincts ran
with blood (B.C. 63).   Twelve thousand Jews perished; and many
priests were cut down at the altar.   But to the Jewish mind the
greatest enormity of all was the sacrilegious act of Pompey in
entering the Holy of Holies.   This he did apparently out of
curiosity, for he abstracted none of the temple treasures.   He
even gave orders for the purification of the sanctuary, and for the
continuance of the legal sacrifices under Hyrcanus II., who was
designated high priest and ethnarch, without the title of king.
The instigators of the war were beheaded, and the country was
made tributary to the Romans.   At one blow the fabric of Jewish
freedom, so laboriously built up, fell down, never to rise again.
This, then, was the outcome of their miserable internal strifes,
and of the insane policy of inviting the interference of strangers.
The spirit of the Maccabees was dead, and the work of a century
annulled.   Judea was once more reduced to the dimensions of a
small shire, and a Roman garrison occupied Jerusalem.   Galilee,
Samaria, the cities to the east of the Jordan, and the maritime
towns, were all taken from the Jews and joined to the Roman
province of Syria.   Pompey then travelled by way of Cilicia, in
order to celebrate his triumph at Rome.   Aristobulus and his
family he carried along with him as prisoners.   The elder son,
Alexander, effected his escape ; but his brother Antigonus, and
his two sisters, had to march beside their father in front of
Pompey's chariot when in B.C. 61 that commander paraded the
streets of the metropolis in all the pomp of victory.   Many other
Jewish captives also were forced to walk in that procession.
These were subsequently set at liberty, and formed the nucleus
of the important Jewish community existing at Rome a century
later.

BOOK VI

THE ROMAN PERIOD, B.C. 63-4

CHAPTER I

THE DOWNFALL OF THE ASMONEANS

1. **Syria under the Romans.**—The power of the Seleucidæ had been destroyed by Pompey in B.C. 65 during his campaign in Asia, and Syria had become a Roman province. As Palestine was still subject to the oversight of the governors of this province, its history continued to be bound up with that of Syria, and began to be a factor in the larger history of Rome. Some account must therefore here be taken of the leading events in the Roman history of the period. In B.C. 60, Cæsar, Pompey, and Crassus formed the so-called First Triumvirate, which was, however, merely a secret compact between themselves. Seven years later, Crassus, after being defeated by the Parthians at Charræ (the ancient Haran), was murdered while attending a conference. He was succeeded in the administration of Syria by Cassius Longinus. Civil war broke out between Cæsar and Pompey in B.C. 49. In August of the year following Pompey was worsted at Pharsalia, and shortly thereafter was assassinated in Egypt. Cæsar now acted as sole dictator, and appointed Sextus Cæsar, one of his own relatives, governor of Syria. But meanwhile many difficulties cropped up in connection with the civil government, and various classes became discontented. At length, in B.C.

44, Cæsar perished through a conspiracy headed by Brutus and
Cassius. Driven from Rome after the funeral oration of Mark
Antony, these two leaders of the republicans hastened to establish,
if possible, their dominion in the East. At Rome there was set
up a new Triumvirate, consisting of Antony, Octavian (grand-
nephew and heir of Cæsar), and Lepidus, the governor of
Narbonese Gaul. Their armies encountered and defeated those
of the conspirators at Philippi in B.C. 42. Brutus and Cassius
both committed suicide. In B.C. 38, Sosius, then governor of Syria,
subdued Antigonus, whom the Parthians had set up as king in
Judea. The new Triumvirate also was to split on the rock of
selfish ambition. First of all Lepidus declared his independence,
but only to be deprived of his province and relegated to private
life. Then heart-burnings arose to alienate Antony and Octavian,
and war broke out between them in B.C. 32. In September of the
next year the decisive battle was fought at Actium, and ended in
the overthrow of Antony. He then fled to Egypt, but in B.C. 30
he was once more defeated by Octavian. After this fresh disaster,
Cleopatra, with whom he had lived a voluptuous life, joined him
in seeking a voluntary death. Left thus without a rival, Octavian
assumed the title of Augustus, and the sovereignty of the Roman
Empire. In B.C. 23 his gifted captain, confidential friend, and
future son-in-law, Agrippa, was sent with large powers to Syria,
which (often by means of legates) he continued to govern for ten
years.

2. **Revival of Patriotic Sentiment among the Jews.**—After having
tasted freedom, the Jewish people were in no mood tamely to
submit themselves to a foreign yoke. Under Pharisaic influence
the national life had no doubt been largely diverted from state-
craft into the peaceful channels of religion and commerce. At no
time had religious thought attained more prominence and strength.
From the legalistic standpoint it was firmly held that Israel was
the people of God, and would experience the fulfilment of the
divine promises through punctilious attention to duty. This idea,

which runs through the whole of the apocalyptic literature subsequent to the Maccabean age, had certainly been well drilled into the public mind. But all this religious zeal did not in the circumstances prevent a wonderful revival of Jewish national feeling. The question, what *was* their duty, still pressed for solution. The ardent spirit of the masses rejected as antiquated the doctrines of the stricter Pharisees, and began to regard patriotic sentiment as a means of realising their Messianic hopes. Their efforts to throw off the Roman dominion they took as the measure of their faith in the promises of God. Men forgot the *religious* character of the Messiah. He was conceived as a temporal prince ; and for the most part the idea of the personal ruler was lost sight of in the anticipation of the temporal kingdom. This could never have happened but for the fact that in Judea Church and State were one. The theocratic views of the people made it impossible for them to separate the thought of the Messiah from that of a victorious earthly king, and caused them to cling to the political idea till it was finally extinguished in the ashes of the Holy City. Formerly, under the Persians, and for a long time under the Greeks also, the Jews were content to bear their political vassalage so long as they had spiritual independence. Now it was otherwise. For a generation they persisted in the struggle for freedom, and earned the reputation of being an unusually intractable and turbulent race.

3. **Ineffectual Efforts of the Asmoneans to assume Power.**—When, accordingly, in A.D. 57, Alexander the son of Aristobulus, who had escaped from the Romans, appeared in Palestine, they were ready to fight in support of his claims to the throne. Hyrcanus II. they looked on as but the tool of Antipater and the Romans. As the accepted representative of the national cause, Alexander soon drove Hyrcanus from Jerusalem, but was hindered by the Roman garrison from rebuilding the walls, which Pompey had demolished. The chief fortresses, however, fell into his hands before Gabinius, now proconsul of Syria, could lead his troops against

him.   Alexander was defeated in the neighbourhood of Jerusalem,
and obliged to fall back on Alexandrium.   Leaving part of his
army to conduct the siege, Gabinius went to superintend the
restoration of Ashdod, Gaza, and other cities devastated by the
Asmonean princes.   This policy was crowned with success, and
earned the gratitude of multitudes.   Out of concern for the
captives at Rome, the mother of Alexander ultimately induced him
to surrender, and on this condition he was set at liberty.

Gabinius now took measures which gave a new political com-
plexion to Palestine, and deprived the Jews of what little freedom
Pompey had left them.   Hyrcanus he restored to Jerusalem, but
committed to him the care of the temple only.   For purposes of
jurisdiction and administration he partitioned the country into five
districts (συνέδρια), each having its own council or Sanhedrin for
the decision of local questions.   The headquarters of these circuits
were Jerusalem, Gadara, Amathus, Jericho, and Sepphoris.   In
vain were these steps taken to weaken the prestige of Jerusalem,
and to destroy the national unity.   The change from a monarchy
to an aristocracy was, however, a popular one, especially with the
inhabitants of the provinces, and with the Pharisees, who had
never approved the attempts made to secure political independence.

In B.C. 56 the Sadducean party made another effort to recover
their lost supremacy.   Aristobulus and his son Antigonus had
escaped from Rome, and had raised a considerable army in
Palestine.   But the insurgents could not cope with the legions of
Gabinius, and Aristobulus, after a brave struggle, in which he
sustained heavy losses, retreated across the Jordan to Machærus.
Covered with wounds, he was forced to surrender after a two days'
siege, and was once more carried a prisoner to Rome.   As
Gabinius now went into Egypt to reinstate the ousted King
Ptolemy XI. Auletes, Antipater took occasion to ingratiate himself with the Roman general by handing over supplies for his
army, and by influencing in his favour the Egyptian Jews located
at Pelusium to guard the frontier.   His services were also requisi-

tioned by Gabinius, when, on returning from Egypt in B.C. 55, he
found Judea again in revolt under Alexander. After Antipater
had brought a number of Jews to submission, Gabinius defeated
Alexander and his 30,000 irreconcilables at Mount Tabor.

In B.C. 54 the triumvir Crassus came to Syria as successor
to Gabinius. To defray the costs of his expedition against the
Parthians, he robbed the temple at Jerusalem ; but soon afterwards both he and his army perished at Carrhæ. This was the
signal for another Jewish rising, which, however, after repulsing
the Parthians, Cassius promptly suppressed. Near the Lake of
Galilee he routed the Jews in battle, and reduced 30,000 of them
to slavery.

On the flight of Pompey and the Senate from Rome in B.C. 49,
Cæsar released Aristobulus from prison in order to send him with
two legions into Syria. Before this plan could be carried out,
however, the adherents of Pompey managed to cut off Aristobulus
by poison ; and about the same time his son Alexander was
beheaded by Scipio at Antioch.

4. Antipater becomes Procurator of Judea.—Although Hyrcanus
II. was nominally head of the Jewish people, he was in reality
only the puppet of Antipater. Nor did the defeat and death of
Pompey break the power of the clever Idumean. His project of
securing the kingdom for his own house could only be realised,
as he clearly perceived, by siding with the Romans, and with
whatever party among the Romans might for the moment be in
the ascendant. Accordingly, after the battle of Pharsalia, this
past master in *finesse* became an active supporter of Julius
Cæsar. In B.C. 47 he rendered valuable service during the
Dictator's campaign against Ptolemy in Egypt. After the war
was ended, Cæsar went to Syria and heaped rewards upon
Hyrcanus and Antipater. In vain did Antigonus, the sole
surviving son of Aristobulus II., appeal to Cæsar to confer the
government upon himself. The only result of his interference
was to benefit still further his opponents   Hyrcanus was now

12

appointed ethnarch of the Jews, with the political power of which
he had been deprived by the five *synedria* of Gabinius; and
Antipater was made procurator of all Judea (*i.e.* including Samaria
and Galilee).

Cæsar wisely granted a large measure of liberty to subject
races; this led them to regard the Roman rule not as an irritating
yoke, but as a defence against enemies. When, therefore, about
this time a golden shield was presented by a Jewish embassy at
Rome, it was cordially accepted, and protection promised to their
country and harbours, just as if Judea had been an independent
State. Moreover, the fast friendship which had sprung up between
Cæsar and Antipater secured many special advantages to the
Jews of Palestine, and also to those of the Diaspora. This was
strikingly shown when, in B.C. 46, as Cæsar was preparing to fight
against Scipio and Cato in Africa, Jewish ambassadors came to
ask for fresh concessions. He ordained that the regulations of
their law as to the annual payment of tribute should be respected,
and that the high priest should have his customary revenues;
that no military burdens should be imposed upon Judea; that the
city of Joppa should be handed over to the Jews as an inheritance
for the high priest; that Lydda and other places which Pompey
had taken from them should be restored; that seats of honour
should be reserved for Hyrcanus and his friends at the gladia-
torial shows in the Roman amphitheatre; and that he should have
special facilities in the matter of approaching the Senate. By
reason of their Sabbath law the Jews were also freed from
military service. Although these privileges were practically the
result of Cæsar's gratitude to Antipater, the Jews chafed under
their growing subjection to the Idumean. He now openly used
threats to enforce his will; and as a step towards making his
power hereditary in his own house, he appointed his eldest son,
Phasael, governor of Jerusalem, and his second son, Herod,
governor of Galilee. These measures excited much hostility
towards him throughout Judea. The Sadducean aristocracy,
who had held influential positions in the *synedria*, exerted them-

selves to make the power of Hyrcanus something more than a name. For once the Pharisees sided with them, and even the indolent Hyrcanus shared the general discontent. The address and courage of his two sons, however, combined with his own ability, enabled Antipater to surmount all difficulties so long as Cæsar was alive ; but not even his foresight could discount such an event as the assassination of "the foremost man in all the world" (B.C. 44). This suddenly threw his machinery out of gear, and made the Jews less inclined than ever to endure the hated domination of the Idumeans. When, therefore, Antipater, true to his uniform policy, transferred his service to the republican cause, and zealously began to collect the exorbitant taxes levied by Cassius, a certain ambitious *protégé* of his, named Malichus, had him secretly poisoned, thinking thereby to preserve Judea for the Jews (B.C. 43). But by this course he overshot the mark ; it caused Antipater to be thought of as a just, pious, and patriotic man, and left the Jews to deal with a greater than Antipater in the person of his distinguished son.

5. **The Sons of Antipater.**—Phasael appears to have shown zeal and tact in managing the affairs of Jerusalem ; but Herod was in every way the stronger of the two brothers, and was destined to leave his mark upon Jewish history. While yet a youth, as governor of Galilee, he had courageously executed the robber-chief Hezekiah. This endeared Herod to the Syrians, and also to the Roman governor, Sextus Cæsar ; but it brought him into collision with the Sanhedrin, which had the sole right to pronounce a death sentence. Hyrcanus was persuaded to summon Herod to answer for his conduct before this body. But the head-strong culprit defied them ; he appeared before his judges clothed in purple and attended by a bodyguard. They were thoroughly cowed, and remained silent. Only one scribe—the famous Shammai—inveighed against the toleration of so scandalous an attempt to overbear justice. After this reproachful speech it would certainly have gone hard with Herod, had not Hyrcanus,

to whom Sextus Cæsar had written ordering his acquittal, weakly adjourned the trial and advised him to escape. Herod accordingly retired to Damascus, and was appointed by Sextus governor of Cœle-Syria. He then advanced with an army against Jerusalem to avenge the affront that had been offered to him ; but his father and his brother, like the relatives of Coriolanus before the walls of Rome, induced him to withdraw his troops.

Shortly after this, in B.C. 46, Sextus was slain and supplanted by Cæcilius Bassus, one of Pompey's adherents. Thereupon, under the successive leadership of Vetus and Murcus (B.C. 45-44), Cæsar's party, aided by Antipater, besieged him in Apamea, but without result. When, however, after the murder of Cæsar, Cassius arrived in Syria, he succeeded in getting both Bassus and Murcus to join him. This gave him supremacy in Syria. In order to maintain his army, he levied taxes on the various towns. No regard was paid to the right of exemption held by the Jews. They were ordered to pay 700 talents, which sum Antipater and his sons, eager to ingratiate themselves with Cassius, as formerly with Cæsar, did their utmost to raise. Herod was the first to hand over his contribution of 100 talents from Galilee, and was reappointed governor.

The murder of Antipater, which took place about this time, although not unwelcome to Hyrcanus, naturally roused the indignation of his own sons. Herod was for taking immediate vengeance, but Phasael persuaded him to wait for a convenient opportunity of dealing with Malichus. When, therefore, the latter simulated sorrow for Antipater's death, the two brothers allowed him to think that his ruse had succeeded. Shortly afterwards, both Herod and Malichus went into Asia Minor to congratulate Cassius on the capture of Laodicea. Malichus repaired to Tyre with the view of rescuing his son, who was living there as a Roman hostage, and of subsequently raising a revolt in Judea. But ere he could execute his designs, he was, at Herod's instigation, stabbed on the seashore by the soldiers of Cassius.

On the departure of Cassius from Syria in B.C. 42, fresh dis-

turbances arose in Judea. Phasael repulsed the Roman general
Felix, and Herod drove the brother of Malichus out of the strongholds. But the two brothers had another enemy to encounter.
Antigonus, the son of Aristobulus II., once more attempted to
assume the sovereignty. He was assisted by his brother-in-law,
Ptolemy Menneus of Chalcis, and by Marion, whom Cassius had
made despot of Tyre. Herod compelled the latter to relinquish
three Galilean fortresses, and earned some popularity by his
generous treatment of the Tyrians. He then marched against
Antigonus, and defeated him on the Jewish frontier. Although
Hyrcanus had sided with Felix against the Idumeans, Herod knew
that, as high priest and heir of the Maccabees, he was still a force
to be reckoned with, and he now astutely betrothed himself to
Mariamne, who, as granddaughter to both Hyrcanus and Aristobulus, united in her own person the two contending branches of
the Asmonean house.

The battle of Philippi, in B.C. 42, secured for Antony the lordship
of Asia. At Bithynia he was met by a crowd of ambassadors.
Among these were some Jewish nobles, who complained that the
government of Hyrcanus was a farce, and that all the power was
in the hands of Phasael and Herod. But Antony, who had been
the friend of Antipater, was easily bribed by Herod to pay no
heed to their accusations. A second deputation, consisting of a
hundred of the most influential Jews, appeared before Antony at
Daphne in Syria to renew their suit. It succeeded no better
than the first. Herod was defended by a certain Messala ; and
Antony, having elicited from Hyrcanus the admission that Herod
and his friends governed the nation best, appointed Phasael and
Herod tetrarchs of Judea (B.C. 41). The reception given to their
deputies at Antioch raised quite a storm in Pharisaic circles.
Although it had already required Herod's intercession to prevent
Antony from putting to death fifteen of his accusers, no fewer
than a thousand Jews assembled on the shore at Tyre, in order to
impeach the Idumeans before him on his arrival in that city.
Antony issued a contemptuous order for their punishment. In

vain did Herod and Hyrcanus implore them to disperse; they were scattered only before the resistless argument of Roman daggers. When they continued their agitation against Herod in the town, Antony wrathfully slew the prisoners whom formerly he had spared.

6. Antigonus set up as King by the Parthians.—In B.C. 40, while Antony remained captivated by Cleopatra in Egypt, the Parthians, led by their prince Pacorus and the satrap Barzapharnes, seized upon Syria. Antigonus promised them 1000 talents and 500 women if they would help him to obtain the kingdom. In two divisions the Parthian troops bore down upon Palestine, and were enthusiastically received by the Jews as deliverers from the thraldom of Herod and the Romans. Herod had but a slender foothold in Jerusalem, and the Sadducean party, allying itself with Antigonus, made a last effort to regain its influence. Pacorus meanwhile arrived at Jerusalem, and induced Hyrcanus and Phasael to walk into a trap. Herod, however, was wily enough to escape by night to Masâda, at the southern end of the Dead Sea. He was, of course, pursued by the Parthians, and so disheartening did the situation appear that he actually meditated suicide. Before gaining the fortress he had to cross swords with the Jews also, whom he defeated on the site of the future citadel of Herodium. After plundering Jerusalem and its environs, the Parthians enthroned Antigonus, and delivered Hyrcanus and Phasael into his hands. The former was taken to Babylonia, after his ears had been cut off, so as to unfit him for the high priest's office, which Antigonus himself assumed under his Hebrew name of Mattathias. Phasael, on the other hand, having heard of Herod's escape, cheerfully killed himself in prison. Supposing his brother to be alive, Herod set out for Petra, in the hope of getting from the Arabian king Malchus money sufficient for his redemption. Malchus, however, through dread of the Parthians, warned him off his territory. He then went to Alexandria, and sailed for Rome. Straightway he poured into the sympathetic

ears of Antony the tale of his misfortunes. Octavian also was
readily induced to take up the cause of Antipater's son, and by
decree of Senate Herod was proclaimed King of Judea. Meanwhile only an opportune rainfall saved Masâda from falling into
the hands of Antigonus, and the Roman general Ventidius and
his lieutenant Silo, who were sent to oust the Parthians, both
accepted bribes from the Jewish pretender. His fortunes were
therefore distinctly on the wane when in B.C. 39 Herod landed
at Ptolemais. But the plundering policy of the Parthians now
led the masses, especially in Galilee, to revert to the Idumean
standard, and Herod soon commanded a large army. Having
taken Joppa, he marched to the relief of his relatives in Masâda,
and finally to Jerusalem itself. Here he met with but a half-
hearted support from Silo and his Roman troops, who first
clamoured for better rations, and then withdrew to winter quarters.
As nothing could be done at Jerusalem, Herod sent his brother
Joseph with an army to Idumea, settled his relatives securely in
Samaria, and marched in person into Galilee. He quickly drove
out the garrison of Antigonus from Sepphoris, and after some
severe fighting subdued the robbers of Arbela.

In spite of all his efforts the ambitious Idumean had as yet
made little headway. The Jews clearly preferred a degenerate
Asmonean to a half-foreigner like Herod. If he was ever to
secure the kingdom, help must come to him from outside. Meanwhile the defeat of the Parthians in B.C. 38 enabled Ventidius to
send auxiliaries to Herod ; but their general Machæras, disap-
pointed in an attempt to master Antigonus by artifice, took to
slaughtering Herodians and Sadducees indiscriminately. It happened that Antony was then present at the siege of Samosata.
Herod, seizing his opportunity, hastened thither, and, after
rendering timely aid to the Romans, received the assurance that
he would be established in his kingdom. Sosius was ordered to
go to his assistance with two legions.

During his absence, however, many disasters befell the cause of
Herod. His brother Joseph had foolishly risked a battle and lost

his life ; the Galileans, again in revolt, had drowned many influential Herodians in the lake ; the disaffection had spread to
Judea ; and Machæras had retired to the fortress of Gitta. These
tidings reached Herod at Daphne. With all haste he marched
into Galilee, which he soon once more subdued. He then proceeded to avenge his brother's death by burning down five
small towns near Jericho, and by the slaughter of 2000 men.
At Isana he routed Pappus, whom Antigonus had sent with an
army against Samaria. As soon as the rigour of winter was past,
he laid siege to Jerusalem, and repeated the tactics of Pompey.
Everything having been thus set in train, Herod calmly proceeded to Samaria, in order to celebrate his marriage with
Mariamne. The event was well timed, for it enabled him to
pose as a sort of champion of the Asmoneans. Returning to
Jerusalem, he was joined by Sosius, and the united armies prosecuted the siege. In spite of the dearth of provisions entailed
by the Sabbatic year, the Jews inside the capital resolved to hold
out to the last. Their courage was sustained by the belief that
the Messianic deliverance was at hand. In five months, however,
the city was taken, and the streets ran with blood. This took
place in June, B.C. 37, on the twenty-sixth anniversary of the
capture of the city by Pompey. By distributing presents to
Sosius and his army, Herod contrived to restrain them from acts
of desecration and plunder. Antigonus fell down cringing at the
feet of Sosius, who contemptuously named him Antigone, and
carried him bound to Antioch, where Antony had him executed
in order to gratify Herod. The latter now obtained the kingdom
which the Roman Senate had made over to him three years previously, and the Asmonean dynasty was at an end.

CHAPTER II

THE REIGN OF HEROD THE GREAT

Herod's family had long been a potent factor in Jewish politics, and had in his person attained its persistent object. But although his own reign was to last for more than a generation, the new dynasty which he had founded scarcely survived himself. The political atmosphere was so charged with electricity as to render a storm inevitable. In the days of his son Archelaus it broke out with fearful intensity. It is hard to say which was the greater—the infamy of many of his proceedings, or the retribution that followed them.

1. **Consolidation of his Power.**—The beginning of Herod's reign was marked by an outburst of cruel selfishness. Forty-five of the leading Sadducean nobles who had been supporters of Antigonus were executed, and their property confiscated; while Pollio (Abtalion) and Sameas (Shammai), the leaders of the Pharisees who had counselled the opening of the city gates during the siege, were raised to honour. Herod was almost compelled by force of circumstances to throw himself into the arms of the Pharisaic party, which in his days reached the height of its prosperity. It was divided into two great schools, those of Shammai and Hillel. The adherents of Shammai advocated the strictest interpretation of the law; those of Hillel held views somewhat more liberal.[1] Only by allying himself with the Pharisees could Herod hope to maintain the security of his throne. He seems to have had a shrewd

---

[1] By his extraordinary thirst for knowledge, combined with a singularly beautiful character, Hillel, who came from Babylon to Jerusalem in extreme poverty, ultimately took precedence of all the Rabbis. It is scarcely surprising that many should have formed an exaggerated estimate of such a man. See Delitzsch's interesting essay on "Jesus and Hillel."

perception of this from the first, when he wisely saved the temple from profanation by the Roman soldiers. He had nothing to hope for from the Sadducees, who, although in many respects more akin to his tastes, were Asmonean partisans ; and he knew that the Pharisees, as standing aloof from politics altogether, would not hinder, if they did not help, his political projects.[1] The consideration shown by Herod for the religious susceptibilities of the Pharisees and Essenes implied no regard on his part for the doctrines which they taught. His adherence to the religion of Israel was purely external and prudential. That he never meant the Pharisaic standpoint to be realised in his kingdom, is shown by his attitude to heathenism. It was his aim to amalgamate pagan forms with Jewish traditions. He surrounded himself with classical influences, and endowed heathen shrines. The ideal he set before himself was to mould his country with the laws of Rome and the spirit of Greece. His Judaism was hardly skin deep ; indeed, there was not a spark of religion in his nature. He followed Antiochus Epiphanes and Aristobulus in disregarding the hereditary character of the high-priestly office, which became a mere appanage of the secular power. Creatures of his own, mostly obscure nonentities from Babylon and Egypt, were set up and removed at pleasure. In this way the power of the old priestly aristocracy was broken, and the Sadducees were reluctantly compelled to abandon politics for controversial discussion on moot points of theological casuistry ; but in this field they were no match for the Pharisees. It was not until after Herod's death that they succeeded in regaining something of their former prestige.

Meanwhile another hostile element had to be dealt with, in the shape of the still surviving Asmoneans. On them, it was quite clear, the national hopes were fixed ; Herod was regarded as the minion of the Romans. His marriage having failed to win for him popular acceptance as the heir of the Asmoneans, Herod's gloomy

---

[1] For active aid in this direction he had to look to the " Herodians "— soldiers or attachés in his Court, whose weapons, however, were diplomatic rather than military.

apprehensions led him, during the earlier years of his reign, to
extirpate one by one the remaining members of that dynasty.
A beginning was made with Aristobulus III., son of Alexander,
and brother of Mariamne. Complications had arisen with reference to the high priesthood. The mutilated Hyrcanus, who had
returned from Babylonia, was no longer eligible ; while Aristobulus III., being only a youth of sixteen, was under the age prescribed by law. Herod nominated for the office one Ananel, a
Babylonian Jew of Aaronic descent, but otherwise of little account.
This was strongly resented by Alexandra, who regarded the
dignity as the birthright of Aristobulus, and wrote to Cleopatra
to bespeak her good offices with Antony in the matter of forcing
Herod to confer the high priesthood on her son. As these representations promised to be effectual, and as he also continued to
be badgered on the subject by his wife, Herod saw nothing for it
but to displace Ananel and give the office to Aristobulus. Both
acts were contrary to the law. Herod's suspicion was now
thoroughly roused, and Alexandra's life was rendered so miserable
by constant espionage, that she determined to escape with her
son to Cleopatra. A servant's treachery enabled Herod to frustrate this design, and he resolved to be rid of Aristobulus. The
enthusiasm of the people for their youthful high priest, on his
appearance at the Feast of Tabernacles, filled the tyrant with a
murderous jealousy. One day he was entertained by Alexandra
at Jericho, Aristobulus also being present. After the banquet,
at Herod's instigation, he joined others who were bathing in the
fish-ponds attached to the house. Some of the king's reptiles
plunged him under water as if in sport, but held him down until
he was drowned (B.C. 35). Herod shed copious tears, gave Aristobulus a magnificent funeral, and reappointed Ananel high priest.
Alexandra, who took in the situation at once, succeeded through
Cleopatra in getting Herod summoned to defend himself before
Antony at Laodicea. With his usual address, however, and by
lavish presents, the Idumean once more ingratiated himself with
the voluptuous Roman, and returned in triumph to Jerusalem.

There fresh troubles awaited him. Before departing, he had given orders to Joseph, his brother-in-law, to slay his wife Mariamne in the event of his own destruction by Antony, so that she might never belong to another. The garrulous Joseph divulged his secret, and on Herod's return Mariamne reproached him with his cruel intentions. This led him to credit some scandalous reports circulated by his mother Cypros and his sister Salome, with the result that he had Joseph executed and Alexander thrown into prison.

A third source of trouble to Herod lay beyond Palestine altogether. The Egyptian Cleopatra coveted his territory, and induced Antony to make over to her some of the most valuable parts of it, including the coast towns and the palm-growing district of Jericho. For these he had to pay tribute to her. Had not his advisers dissuaded him, he would at this time have assassinated Cleopatra, who visited Palestine on her way back from Armenia, whither she had accompanied Antony. As it was, he received her with every mark of friendship, and escorted her to Egypt, while studiously eluding her wiles. The great war between Octavian and Antony being now at hand, Herod prepared an auxiliary force to aid the latter. Antony, however, urged by Cleopatra, ordered him to invade Arabia and punish Malchus for non-payment of tribute. By thus setting her two vassals against each other, the queen of Egypt hoped to weaken the power of both; but, after a severe struggle, the Arabians were forced to acknowledge the lordship of Herod.

The defeat of Antony by Octavian at Actium was a serious thing for the Jewish king. It meant that the world had a new master, and that master one whom he had opposed. But Herod knew how to play a desperate game. First of all he removed Hyrcanus from his path (B.C. 30). At such a crisis he could not brook the thought of a possible rival, however old and feeble. The general conduct of affairs he committed to his brother Pheroras. His mother, sister, and family he placed in the stronghold of Masâda. Mariamne and Alexandra were located at Alexandrium, under the charge of two trusty men, Joseph and Soemus, who were enjoined to slay them both should any mischief befall himself. Having thus put his house in order, Herod appeared before the conqueror in Rhodes. Upon his frankly stating that he had deserted Antony not because of his defeat, but because he refused to recover his fortunes by killing Cleopatra, Augustus at once re-established him in his kingdom. Soon after, Herod entertained his new patron with royal magnificence at Ptolemais, and supplied the wants of his army. Augustus was not long in gaining a victory in Egypt, where both Antony and Cleopatra committed suicide. Herod hastened to meet him, and received as a present not only Cleopatra's bodyguard, together with all the territory of which she had deprived him, but also Gadara, Hippos, Samaria, Gaza, Anthedon, Joppa, and Strato's Tower.

All this public success was neutralised by domestic misery. Chafing under what was practically imprisonment, provoked at the wilful murder of her kinsmen, and once more aware of his cruel purpose regarding herself, Mariamne received her husband with haughty resentment. Herod's mother and sister did all they could to foster the discord between the unhappy pair. They bribed the king's cup-bearer to accuse Mariamne of an attempt to poison him. Her eunuch confessed under torture that she hated her husband because of his injunctions to Soemus. Herod took this as a proof of his wife's infidelity, and immediately put Soemus to death. A packed jury condemned Mariamne, and she too was led to execution in B.C. 29. As soon as she was dead, Herod was seized with remorse, and vainly resorted first to feasting and then to hunting in order to drown his grief. Presently he fell ill at Samaria. As his physicians seemed unable to cope with the disease, Alexandra attempted to get possession of the two strongholds in Jerusalem, with the view of controlling the succession to the throne. When Herod heard of this he ordered her execution (B.C. 28). Not content with having cleared out of the way the last descendant of the Asmonean house, the bloodthirsty monster contrived to slay all who for any reason were obnoxious to him.   There perished thus the Idumean Costobarus, Salome's second husband, and a number of his confederates.   After the execution of these persons in B.C. 25, there no longer remained anyone to endanger Herod's power.

2. Herod's Promotion of Pagan Culture. — Once secure in his kingdom, Herod began in various ways to gratify his own peculiar tastes, and to pose as the friend of the Romans. Affecting to be a man of culture, he brought to his Court Greek scholars and artists, honoured them with his friendship, conferred upon them important offices of State, and even became their pupil in philosophy and rhetoric.   To this learned circle belonged the historian Nicolaus of Damascus and his brother Ptolemy ; another Ptolemy, who was custodian of the royal seal ; Andromachus and Gemellus, who acted as tutors to Herod's sons; and Irenæus the orator.   Except that he abstained from violence, Herod's introduction of foreign practices into Palestine was such as to recall the times of Antiochus Epiphanes.   A theatre embellished with the trophies of nations vanquished by Augustus, and also an amphitheatre, were erected at Jerusalem.   Festal games were held every fifth year in honour of Cæsar.   Other nations were invited to take part in the contests.   These included racing and wrestling, wild-beast fights and shows, musical competitions, and other exercises familiar to the Roman arena. Dispirited by recent calamities, the mass of the Jewish people feebly acquiesced in this subversion of their country's law ; but the more sober among them detested these sports as heathenish innovations.   Ten citizens of Jerusalem even conspired to murder Herod in the theatre ; they were, however, betrayed and executed. Soon after the informer was lynched, and Herod must have perceived how welcome his death would have been to his subjects. As a protection against their hatred, he began to cover the land with fortresses, and to maintain an organised espionage.   Outside the limits of Judea, he erected pagan temples and endowed com-

petitive games. In many instances he undertook costly enter-
prises beyond Palestine altogether. When the temple of Apollo
at Rhodes was burnt down, he rebuilt it at his own expense.
Gymnasiums at Tripoli, Damascus, and Ptolemais ; temples and
market-places at Berytus and Tyre ; theatres at Sidon and
Damascus ; baths and fountains at Ascalon ; colonnades at
Antioch ; and a piazza at Chios, rose as monuments of his
liberality. He also buttressed up the declining revenues of the
Olympic games. His transparently thin apology for these gifts
to heathen shrines and foreign cities was that as the vassal of the
Romans he was obliged to consult their wishes rather than his
own. The truth is that he was in no real sense a Jew, and that
behind the flimsy pretext of honouring the Romans he was
indulging his own vainglorious ambition.

3. Herod's Passion for Building.—At first this took the strictly
utilitarian form of erecting fortresses. The ancient citadel of
Baris was rebuilt and called Antonia ; Samaria, Strato's Tower,
Gaba in Galilee, and Heshbon in Perea, were all fortified and
garrisoned. Well-known strongholds like Alexandrium, Hyrcania,
Machærus, and Masâda were splendidly restored. Of the other
citadels built by Herod, two were named Herodium after himself,
and one Cypros in honour of his mother. Many new cities also,
built on the Roman model, owed their existence to his enterprise.
One, situated in the valley of the Jordan, was called Phasaelis in
memory of his brother. Capharsaba and Anthedon were reconstructed under the new names of Antipatris and Agrippæum.
A spacious royal palace was built at Jerusalem in the upper city,
and its main wings bore the names of Cæsar and Agrippa. Outside of Judea proper, two cities especially had reason to congratulate themselves upon his favour. These were Samaria and
Strato's Tower. On being reconstructed, they both received new
names in honour of the Roman emperor ; Samaria was called
Sebaste (Augusta), and Strato's Tower, Cæsarea. The former
was considerably enlarged, and enclosed by a splendid wall

twenty furlongs in length. In the middle of the city, within a
sacred grove, there towered a great Samaritan temple dedicated
to Cæsar. Herod's operations at Cæsarea were on a still grander
scale. Twelve years were spent by him in erecting this maritime
capital of Judea, which then stood forth as an embodiment of the
magnificence of his conceptions. At vast expense, on a seaboard
singularly destitute of safe harbours, he constructed a haven
rivalling the Piræus at Athens. Overlooking the harbour, and
visible far out on the Mediterranean, rose the temple of Cæsar.
Cæsarea could also boast of a substantial theatre, amphitheatre,
and market-place. The completion of the city was celebrated
with fitting pomp in the year B.C. 10.

Herod's crowning architectural achievement, however, was the
rebuilding of the temple at Jerusalem. Zerubbabel's temple,
dwarfed as it was by many of the newer buildings, was no longer
suitable for the headquarters of Judaism. Besides, a monarch
who had gratuitously equipped so many pagan temples in
Hellenistic towns within his own dominions, could scarcely fail to
do something for the great Jewish sanctuary. His proposal was
nevertheless received with such suspicion, that he had to delay
commencing the work until all the materials for it were collected
and prepared. Then at last the old foundations were removed.
A thousand priests were specially trained as masons and carpenters, so that only sacred hands should rear the temple. It was
built with huge blocks of white marble. Its length was 100 cubits,
and its greatest height 120 cubits—dimensions exceeding those
of Solomon's temple. The internal arrangements were practically those of the previous structures. The eastern entrance was
hung with embroidered curtains, over which was emblazoned a
golden vine as an emblem of God's favour (cf. Ps. lxxx. 8). The
building of the temple proper was commenced in B.C. 20, and
finished within a year and a half. It was then consecrated with
great éclat on the anniversary of Herod's enthronement. Eight
years more were devoted to the erection of splendid porticoes ;
indeed, building operations were still being carried on in the time

of Christ. The sacred edifice was garnished throughout with the spoils of vanquished nations. Over the outer forecourt was an inscription, forbidding foreigners to enter under pain of death. The inner temple, the space around the altar, and the cloisters of the priests, were inaccessible to Herod himself, who was not of sacerdotal descent. His erection of a golden eagle over the great gate of the temple, however, neutralised all his concessions to Pharisaism. This was not a mere case of pandering to Rome; it was an affront to Judaism, and resented as such. But Herod was the last man to care for religious consistency.

4. Herod as a Ruler.—In his foreign policy he was conspicuously successful. It was a fixed principle with him to maintain friendly relations with Rome, and to this worldly-wise attitude he owed much of the external splendour of his reign. Herod lost no opportunity of cultivating the friendship of Augustus and his son-in-law, Agrippa. In their expeditions he was always ready to assist them. Thus it came about that in the emperor's estimation Herod stood next to Agrippa, and in Agrippa's next to Augustus. His sons were sent to Rome for their education. Augustus showed his appreciation of these civilities by adding to Herod's territory the districts of Trachonitis, Batanea, and Auranitis, and subsequently the valuable regions of Ulatha and Paneas, at the sources of the Jordan. Near Paneas Herod built a splendid temple, which he dedicated to Cæsar. He also now got his brother Pheroras appointed tetrarch of Perea, and was himself associated with the procurators of Syria, whose administration was made subject to his approval. Through his influence with the Romans a new position was also won for Judaism in the eyes of the pagan world.

Far less satisfactory was his administration in Judea itself. Not that it lacked its good points. The utility of some of his public works was unquestionable, and his *régime* was favourable to commerce. He once remitted a third of the burdensome taxation, and at another time a fourth. Towards the close of his reign he placed 3000 Idumean colonists in Trachonitis to check the robber tribes in that region. During a famine in B.C. 24 he parted with his rich furniture and plate. The money thus realised he sent to Petronius, governor of Egypt, and received in return supplies of corn, which were freely distributed among the poor. Clothing was similarly furnished during the winter, and extensive gifts of seed were bestowed on Jews and Syrians alike. These liberal and energetic measures did much to restore general prosperity, and even to reconcile some of his bitterest enemies. But his popularity was short-lived. No generosity could atone for his offences against the law. One of the worst of these was his expulsion from the high priesthood of Jesus the son of Phabet, in order to confer the dignity upon Simon the son of Bœthus, whose daughter Mariamne he had married. He also enacted that thieves should be sold out of the kingdom. This high-handed procedure roused the rebellious instincts of the people; but Herod took refuge in a very thoroughgoing police system. The right of public meeting was withheld; dangerous persons were taken to the citadel Hyrcania and put to death; spies everywhere kept a sleepless watch; even the king himself, like James V. of Scotland in a later age, went about in disguise in order to ascertain how his subjects were affected towards him. An oath of fidelity was exacted from all except certain Pharisees who had been of service to him, and the gentle Essenes, one of whom, Menahem by name, had even in Herod's boyhood predicted that he would be king of the Jews. These last were but slight and exceptional exhibitions of clemency, and cannot appreciably affect the character of a reign which for vengeful purpose, selfish cruelty, tyrannical despotism, and wanton bloodshed, has happily few parallels in history.

5. **Last Years of Herod.**—Herod reigned in all thirty-three years. The first twelve (B.C. 37–25) were spent in fighting his way to power; during the next twelve (25–13) he ruled in all his glory; the last nine (13–4) formed an ignoble period of family cruelties. He was now to suffer a poetic retribution for the crimes of his earlier days. The slayer of the Asmoneans became the slayer

of his own sons ; his heart became a hell within, his home a howling wilderness, and his whole existence a nightmare.

About the year 18 B.C., when their studies had been completed, Herod went to fetch his sons Alexander and Aristobulus from Rome. Their mother's looks and royal bearing had been transmitted to the two young men, and the people recognised this with delight. But the jealousy of Salome was aroused, and she began to plot against them as she had plotted against Mariamne. It was given out that it was repulsive to them to live with their mother's murderer. For a time, however, Herod paid no heed to these rumours, and married Aristobulus to Berenice, Salome's own daughter, and Alexander to Glaphyra, the daughter of Archelaus, king of Cappadocia. In B.C. 15, Agrippa visited Judea and offered sacrifices in the temple at Jerusalem. The visit was returned by Herod in the spring of the following year. He met Agrippa at Sinope in Pontus, and assisted him in his campaign at the Bosphorus. Thereafter the two friends travelled through Asia Minor, and at Herod's instigation Agrippa confirmed the Jews inhabiting those parts in the observance of their national customs.

Meanwhile in Herod's household things had been going from bad to worse. Salome and Pheroras hated the young men, and tried to inflame them against their father ; the youths themselves undisguisedly disliked these Idumeans. On Herod's return, Salome and Pheroras hinted that his sons were on the point of avenging their mother's death. Suspicious and alarmed, the king took the worst of all plans to prove to these proud-spirited youths that their succession to the throne was not a foregone conclusion. He brought back to his Court his first wife Doris, and her son Antipater, towards whom he began to show a marked partiality. Mariamne's sons resented this ; Antipater, on the other hand, made the most of his position. By adroitly flattering his father and calumniating his half-brothers he contrived to widen the breach between them. At the same time he wormed himself more and more into favour with Herod, who sent him to Rome in

the company of Agrippa, with every recommendation to Cæsar.
Even from the Roman Court this wretch continued to send stories
fitted to increase his father's jealousy against the two guileless
youths. At last Herod accused them before Augustus at Aquileia.
They were declared innocent, and a reconciliation was effected on
the understanding that their father should have power to nominate
his successor. On his arrival at Jerusalem, Herod addressed an
assembly in the temple, claimed for himself the rights of ruler
while he lived, and nominated as his successors his three sons,
Antipater, Alexander, and Aristobulus, in the order of seniority.

Soon afterwards Herod's cupidity led him to plunder the
sepulchres of David and Solomon. Conscience-stricken on
account of this sacrilege, and anxious to magnify the history of
his nation, he proceeded to erect a splendid marble monument
over the ancient graves. These exploits were followed by fresh
outbreaks of strife in his family. Antipater's profession of
pleasure at the reconciliation between Herod and the sons of
Mariamne was a piece of hypocrisy. Aided by Pheroras and
Salome, he still continued his cunning intrigues, until the
atmosphere of the Jewish Court became rank with suspicion
and invective. Alexander's sayings were communicated by spies
to Antipater, who in turn brought garbled versions of them to
Herod. This "mystery of iniquity" further inflamed the king's
jealousy by apologising for Alexander. Herod now became a
terror to his own domestics and adherents; his palace was
turned into a wild beast's lair. Servants were tortured, and old
friends expelled. Only one poor creature on the rack could be
got to compromise Alexander, who was then thrown into chains.
With the recklessness of despair the prisoner wrote to Herod,
incriminating not only himself but also many of the king's most
faithful friends. At this critical stage King Archelaus happily
appeared upon the scene, and with great tact and wisdom poured
oil upon the waters.

It was now Herod's misfortune to incur the displeasure of
Cæsar. During his absence in Rome the inhabitants of

Trachonitis had once more risen in rebellion. Although defeated by his generals, about forty of the ringleaders retreated to a place of safety provided by the Arabian minister Syllæus, to whom he had refused Salome in marriage. In concert with the Roman governors in Syria, Herod demanded the cession of the robbers. Syllæus meanwhile went to Rome to lodge a complaint against Herod. The Jewish king, however, invaded Arabia, demolished the robber fortress of Raepta, and transported 3000 Idumeans to Trachonitis. Syllæus presented an aggravated report of these proceedings to Augustus, who wrote to Herod in terms of strong disapproval. The attitude of both the Arabians and the people of Trachonitis immediately became more defiant, and on the death of King Obodas things were in a state of anarchy throughout Arabia and Judea. Herod had already sent ambassadors to Rome to plead his cause, but in vain. He now despatched his historiographer-royal, Nicolaus of Damascus, to answer the charge laid against him. Nicolaus very cleverly turned the tables upon Syllæus, who was condemned to death ; through his able advocacy Herod was also reinstated in the royal favour.

In the Jewish Court the old sores had broken out afresh. The former conspirators were reinforced by a disreputable Spartan, Eurykles, who flattered Alexander to his face and slandered him to Antipater. Every calumny reached the ears of Herod, who became implacable in his hatred of his sons, and put to torture all whom he considered likely to compromise them. Nothing could be elicited, however, beyond the fact that they had resolved to flee to King Archelaus. That monarch again did his best to restore harmony, but in vain. The jealous tyrant kept the youths in fetters and apart, while letters were carried to the emperor charging them with treason. Augustus allowed Herod a free hand in dealing with his sons, but advised that the case should be judicially tried at Berytus. The decision was against the young men, who were not permitted to appear for themselves ; they were condemned to death. The whole nation now waited to see whether the sentence would be carried out. An old soldier, Teron, openly protested, and even privately remonstrated with the king.   On the other hand, Trypho, the king's barber, accused Teron of having urged him to cut Herod's throat ; whereupon Teron and his son, the barber, and 300 other suspects, were stoned to death.   The last act in the tragedy speedily followed.   About the year 7 B.C., Herod ordered Alexander and Aristobulus to be strangled at Sebaste, where their mother Mariamne had become his bride.   No wonder Augustus caustically declared that he would rather be Herod's pig than his son !

Antipater had now got rid of his rivals, but only to become the object of general hatred.   His father associated him with himself in the government of the nation, and in deference to his wishes even altered his plans of marriage for the children of the slaughtered Asmoneans—indulgences which this monster of a son repaid by scheming for his removal.   It was part of his plan to lavish gifts on Herod's influential Roman friends, whose good-will was essential to the fulfilment of his hopes.   He had also private cabals with Pheroras, while in public he always opposed him.   But the lynx-eyed Salome, who at Herod's instance had married his friend Alexas, soon detected what was going on, and reported everything to the king.   Special blame was thus attached to the wife of Pheroras.   In the circumstances Antipater thought it advisable to pay a visit to Rome.   Prior to his departure, Herod provided him with a document settling the succession upon himself, and afterwards upon Herod, son of Mariamne, the high priest's daughter.   As Pheroras refused to part with his wife, both were ordered to leave the kingdom. They retired to Perea, where shortly afterwards Pheroras died. This proved the ruin of Antipater.   On receiving a hint that his brother had been poisoned, Herod had the matter fully investigated.   The first result was to incriminate Antipater's mother. It also turned out that Antipater, with the complicity of his uncle Theudio, had sent poison to Pheroras in order that he might administer it to Herod while he was in Rome.   This discovery involved others also. Mariamne's son Herod was disinherited; she herself was expelled from the palace; and Simon her father was deprived of the priesthood, which was conferred upon one Matthias. The application of torture to the women of Pheroras' household brought out several damaging particulars as to the conversation of Antipater at those midnight meetings. It happened also that another emissary of Antipater's arrived with more poison for his father, and with forged letters full of slanders against Archelaus and Philip. Herod's one desire now was to get this arch-plotter into his hands. Although seven months had elapsed since his crimes were discovered, he was still in the dark about the matter. When, therefore, Herod asked him to return to Jerusalem, he unsuspectingly complied. Everyone shrank from him as a toad. Herod denounced him as the murderer of his brothers, and ordered him to stand his trial next day before Quintilius Varus. His unblushing impudence could not deliver him; Herod put him in chains, and wrote to Cæsar for advice. Antipater's guilt was still more clearly exposed by a slanderous letter purporting to have been written by Salome to the Empress Julia, but in reality forged by himself and sent to Herod by Acme, Julia's maid, whom he had bribed.

The king was now an old man of seventy, enduring the remorseful agonies of one who perceived that he had slain his children for nought. His miseries induced a severe bodily illness, which never left him. He was, besides, greatly disliked. The consciousness that the nation would be relieved to hear of his death served only to increase his native ferocity. Emboldened by the news that his trouble must prove fatal, two popular Rabbis, Judas the son of Sariphäus, and Matthias the son of Margaloth, incited their pupils to pull down the heathenish image from the main entrance to the temple. In broad daylight they hacked in pieces the golden eagle. From his couch at Jericho Herod sentenced forty of the delinquents to be burnt alive.

His own struggle with death was daily becoming more

desperate. In vain he repaired to the warm baths of Callirrhöe beyond Jordan. On his return to Jericho he summoned the elders from every village in Palestine, shut them up in the hippodrome, and gave instructions to Salome and her husband Alexas to have them all slain as soon as he expired, that so there might be lamentation all over the land. This diabolical idea, however, was not carried out. Herod's last pleasure was the receipt of letters from Rome empowering him to deal with Antipater as he thought fit. A false rumour of his father's death led that scheming scoundrel to offer a bribe to his keeper with the view of regaining his freedom. Herod then ordered his execution, and nominated Archelaus king of Judea, Antipas tetrarch of Galilee and Perea, and Philip tetrarch of Trachonitis and the neighbouring region. On the fifth day after the execution of Antipater, in the year B.C. 4, he breathed his last, and was buried with pomp at Herodium.

The surname of "the Great" cannot be applied to Herod without qualification. He merits it only as one of the most prominent personalities of his age, and relatively to his own descendants of the same name. Physically, he was strong, active, and capable of much endurance; mentally, he was shrewd, cunning, and tenacious of purpose; morally, he was passionate, selfish, and ambitious. The one thing he cared for and pursued with unwearied energy was the extension of his own power and glory. His reign presents a strange combination of splendour and misery. In Herod we see a king—

> "Feastful and fearful; ever ill-content
> 'Mid plots and perils; girt with singing boys
> And dancing girls of Tyre, and armoured noise
> Of Caesar's legionaries." [1]

6. **The Advent of Christ.**—At length we turn over the blank leaf between the Old Testament and the New. The opening chapters of the Gospel narrative tell of the birth of Jesus Christ

[1] Sir Edwin Arnold, *The Light of the World.*

at Bethlehem, and throw a lurid light upon one tragic episode of Herod's last days not elsewhere recorded. In the story of the slaughter of the Innocents, the suspicious, cruel, and unscrupulous character of the tyrant shows itself once more. But the same year that saw Christ born (B.C. 4)[1] saw Herod buried. The false glitter of the Idumean paled before the true glory of the Nazarene whose kingdom is not of this world.

The Jews had waited so long for the Messiah that many had ceased to cherish the hope of His coming. But all through these centuries of struggle and vicissitude there had also been shining the spiritual light of the truly pious who waited for the consolation of Israel. A nation's life is never entirely made up of selfish schemers, unprincipled politicians, and fighting ecclesiastics. "The middle ages of sacred history" were sometimes dark enough, yet even then God had not left Himself without witness. In the virgin mother, in the parents of the forerunner, in the group that gathered round the cradle of the infant whose advent brought the great Renaissance for which a still unconscious world was weary, there is disclosed to us the fairest type of pure religion. It had never been extinct. Over every mile of the devious road from the Exile to the Advent, holy hands had held the torch of piety.

The names associated with the direct revelation of the Messiah are not those of earth's mighty ones ; they are those of the men and women who then represented true godliness in Israel. The simple shepherds who tended their flocks on the plains of Bethlehem ; the aged Simeon who devoutly searched the Scriptures for their testimony regarding the Christ ; the prophetess Anna who

---

[1] Herod's death is known to have occurred between 13th March and 4th April in the year of Rome 750. As the Nativity was *prior* to this event (Matt. ii. 1-9), the universally accepted modern chronology, which places the birth of Christ in A.U.C. 754, is wrong by *at least* four years. Thus, assuming that Jesus was born on the 25th of December, the twentieth century really begins not later than December 25th, 1896. This anachronism, due to Dionysius Exiguus, the Roman abbot of the sixth century who introduced the Christian era, cannot now be remedied ; and hence we are shut up to the apparent paradox that our Lord was born in the year B.C. 4.

literally dwelt in the house of the Lord ;—these, and others like-minded, were looking for redemption in Jerusalem, and while yet they looked it came. But not by the wonder and adoration of such alone was the child Jesus encircled ; the Gentile world also laid its tribute of wealth and learning at His feet. Wise men from the East, sharing the general feeling of expectancy then abroad, and led on by a bright temporary star, came to present their gifts and their homage. This act foreshadowed the all-embracing nature of the Messianic kingdom, in which "there is neither Greek nor Jew, circumcision nor uncircumcision, bar-barian, Scythian, bond nor free ; but Christ is all, and in all."

INDEX

203

14